THE HEALTHY LOW-CARB
SLOW COOKER COOKBOOK

the healthy low-carb slow cooker cookbook

100 EASY RECIPES TO KICK-START WEIGHT LOSS

Photography by Marjia Vidal

Shannon Epstein

ROCKRIDGE
PRESS

Cover Designer: Katy Brown
Interior Designer: Brooke Johnson
Photo Art Director: Karen Beard
Editor: Stacy Wagner-Kinnear
Production Editor: Erum Khan

Photography © Marija Vidal, 2018
Author photo © Joshua Monesson, Monesson Photography

Cover: Thai Chicken Tacos, p. 78

ISBN: Print 978-1-64152-317-2| eBook 978-1-64152-318-9

To my followers.
This one is for you.

contents

introduction

After writing two slow cooker cookbooks and a blog called Fit Slow Cooker Queen, it's no secret that I love to cook healthy recipes in my slow cooker. The "Fit" part of my blog is a reference to how I try to live a healthy lifestyle—mainly by cooking healthy food. That's right, food. You can't out-exercise a bad diet!

While I don't follow a particular diet, I tend to naturally eat low-carb foods because of personal preference—mostly lean meats, vegetables, and cheese. I first started paying attention to what I ate after I noticed that, as I was aging, my metabolism started slowing down. It became more difficult to maintain control over my weight. With my 40th birthday officially on the horizon, I found that the things that had always worked for me just didn't work any longer. In the past I could eat moderate amounts of starches, like potatoes or sweet potatoes, at each meal and still easily maintain a healthy weight. Unfortunately, those days were over. I knew I had to make a change, so I started looking for another way to keep my weight down while still eating the foods I loved.

Enter low-carb eating. I'm the first to admit that transitioning to low-carb can be tricky. Carbs are found in more foods than just pasta and rice; they're also in fruits, vegetables, nuts, and more, so it's important to educate yourself. Start reading labels and learn what you can and cannot eat. But, believe me, it is worth it when you realize how much great food is actually low-carb. And you can eat it and still watch the weight drop off.

Once I figured out how I wanted to eat, I had to think about how I was going to cook it. This is where the good old slow cooker comes in handy (or perhaps the Slow Cook function on your brand-new Instant Pot®). Most people live busy lives and it's hard to slow down and make a home-cooked meal. The slow cooker lets you fit that into your life. Since I started using a slow cooker to make my meals, I've discovered that eating healthy is not only easy, but it sure tastes good, too, and that's what I show you in this book. Many of the foods you can eat on a low-carb diet are those that a slow cooker cooks particularly well, like beef, egg casseroles, and hearty soups. The recipes I've created are easy to make, and they use ingredients that are easy to find at the grocery store. You probably already have a lot of them in your pantry. I'm willing to bet there aren't any ingredients in here that are unknown to you. The recipes are a mixture of new and classic dishes, many that you've heard of and some that you'd never guess could be low-carb. Soups, casseroles, seafood, vegetarian entrées, desserts— they're all here, and you'll find making and eating them to be a pleasure. What you won't find are high-carb meals built around ingredients that often find their way into slow cooker recipes, such as legumes and grains.

Sure, diets can be hard to stick to, but think of low-carb eating as a lifestyle adjustment made easier by your slow cooker. With this cookbook, you're one step closer to attaining (and maintaining) your health goals.

cooking low & slow

Slow cookers are all about convenience. And eating foods with fewer carbohydrates, for many, paves a clear path to weight loss. So, I'm pretty excited to combine the two for you here. Slow cookers give you more control over what you're making because you control the ingredients going in, and frankly, natural ingredients cook better in the slow cooker than processed foods. Fresh or even frozen vegetables cook well in a slow cooker and are, in many cases, low in carbs, so you'll see a lot of vegetables in the recipes in this book. Pretty much any cut of meat will work, too; in fact, the tougher the cut, the better it cooks using this method (and tougher cuts are less expensive, so it's a win-win).

Low-Carb Love

Eating a low-carb diet might be the rage these days, but it isn't anything new. People have been eating low-carb foods in an effort to lose weight for years. But over the past few years, other plans, like the paleo diet and the keto diet, have gotten a lot of fanfare online and on social media and have distracted people from a basic low-carb diet plan—a method of eating that has quietly and consistently continued to help people lose weight. When you follow a low-carb diet, you're mainly reducing the amount of starches and sugars that you consume, which are stored as fat in the body. When you avoid foods that contain them, your body stops storing fat and starts using it as fuel. As long as the amount of carbs and calories you eat is kept in check, you will start to shed the weight. Remember, even if you cut back on the carbs, you won't lose weight if you keep consuming the same inflated number of calories.

Healthy Low-Carb Eating

The term *healthy* can mean one thing to one person and another thing to the next. To be clear, we're not eliminating all carbs here. Some are necessary for the healthy functioning of our bodies. Not all carbohydrates affect our bodies the same way. You'll want to avoid such carbohydrates as refined starches and added sugars. The reason is because they can affect blood sugar levels more radically, and can be converted to fat stores in our body more easily, than complex carbohydrates that are found in foods like vegetables. This might sound crazy, but if you're trying to lose fat, you *can* eat fats that are considered better for you. Yes, some fat is good! Avocados are a good example, along with the fats found in fish, nuts, nut butters, and seeds.

KETO, PALEO, WHOLE30®, OH MY

You may have heard of a few diets that are very popular right now: the ketogenic diet (keto), the paleo diet, and the Whole30 diet. Paleo and Whole30 are similar to each other in the sense that they both restrict gluten, grains, refined sugar, artificial sweeteners, preservatives, and overly processed and refined foods. Many people who are looking to cut out processed foods and reduce their intake of unprocessed, naturally high-carb foods (such as grains and legumes) find themselves turning to one of these diets at some point. The keto diet focuses on lowering carbs but in combination with a higher percentage of good fat.

The low-carb approach I talk about in this book is less restrictive than those diets while still encouraging weight loss. And many of the recipes can be easily converted to those diets.

Keto: This is commonly known as a low-carb, high-fat diet. The goal of following a ketogenic diet is to switch your body to burn stored fat, which results in weight loss. Insulin levels become very low, and fat burning increases dramatically. It becomes easy to access your fat stores to burn them off. The goal is to move your body into ketosis by getting your body to burn fatty acids for energy instead of carbohydrates. By cutting carbs from your diet and consuming a moderate amount of protein and a higher amount of natural fats, you will train your body to burn fat for energy instead

of storing it. On this diet, the goal is to keep daily net carbs below 50 grams, though some say carb intake should be as low as 20 grams for optimum results. The basic diet is a mix of protein (meat or seafood), natural fats (olive oil, butter), and most vegetables. Foods to avoid on this diet include potatoes, fruit, gluten, sugar, and legumes.

Paleo: Some call this the "caveman" diet because the foods included in the diet are those that might have been consumed by people during the Paleolithic period. Here you'll be eating only what could be hunted or gathered in that era: meats, fish, fruits, vegetables, nuts, and seeds—nothing processed and nothing refined. Because this diet allows fruits and vegetables that have larger quantities of carbohydrates, lowering carbs is not the focus of this plan.

Whole30: Developed by Melissa Hartwig, this is a temporary elimination diet that's designed to isolate and identify foods that might be causing a variety of ailments. The idea is to cut foods out of your diet that might trigger digestive problems, allergies, inflammation, or chronic pain. The diet starts by cutting out all sugar, alcohol, grains, legumes, dairy, and processed foods. After following the diet for 30 days, some foods are added back to the diet as a way to identify what foods are the cause of discomfort. Although by nature the diet tends to be low-carb, there are no guidelines for how many carbs you should consume.

TOTAL CARBS AND NET CARBS

So far, I've used only the terms *carbohydrates* and *carbs*. You may have heard of "net" carbs or even "active" or "impact" carbs. They all refer to the same thing, and while there is no formal definition, net carbs are generally calculated as the total grams of carbohydrates in a recipe or food product minus the fiber and/or the sugar alcohols. But these numbers can be misleading, because even though fiber and sugar alcohol have a minimal impact on blood sugar levels, in some cases, certain types and amounts may still be converted to glucose. So, look at the total amount of carbohydrates on food labels or in recipes when carb counting to get the most accurate measure of what you are eating. Every recipe in the book includes nutritional content, including total carbs. If you are counting net carbs, make sure to remove fiber grams from the carbs noted.

CARBS AND WEIGHT LOSS

Obviously, our bodies are all different. In order to lose weight, most people need to keep carbohydrates under 50 grams per day while still staying within the recommended daily calorie range. If you keep carbs to 50 grams but eat a lot more protein and fat, you could be essentially eating more calories than you're burning and ultimately not lose weight. As a result, it's important to choose foods that have a low carb count with a high nutritional value without being too high in calories. Try to eat unprocessed, whole foods. Although I've included nutritional values, such as calories, fat, carbohydrates, and protein, for each recipe, they will vary somewhat based on the ingredients and brands you purchase. I encourage you to think about counting carbs in ranges versus exact numbers.

Please keep in mind that the information I share in this cookbook is not intended to be a substitute for informed and personalized medical advice or care. Consult a physician or dietitian before beginning a weight-loss program or other dietary regimen.

SLOW COOKING LOW-CARB FOODS

There are a few things to take into consideration when it comes to low-carb eating and slow cooking in particular. Not all food is suitable for slow cooking. Because slow cookers cook foods at low temperature over a long period, the results can be melt-in-your-mouth meats but also mushy or overcooked vegetables. Chicken breasts are the prime example. Most people think of chicken breasts as the healthier option over chicken thighs, which can be true because thighs are higher in calories and fat. But white meat is very easy to overcook and dry out, so it should be avoided when cooking with a slow cooker. Refer to these lists of which foods you can enjoy and which to avoid.

Foods ideal for low-carb slow cooking:
Dark-meat poultry, ground beef, pork, lamb, cabbage, kale, eggplant, green beans, bell peppers, mushrooms, broccoli, spaghetti squash, tomatoes, zucchini, cauliflower, butternut squash, pumpkin, onions, dairy products, coconut milk, butter, cream

Foods not recommended for low-carb slow cooking:
Tender steaks (rib-eye and tenderloin), rice, pasta, potatoes, beans, peas, lentils, corn

Other foods to avoid:
All grains, legumes, most fruits (except for certain berries), fruit juices, sugars, natural sweeteners (like maple syrup and honey), refined oils (like canola, safflower, and corn oil)

Making Low-Carb Easy

Cooking low-carb might include a bit of a learning curve. Since you're staying away from processed, manufactured foods, you'll be cooking a lot from scratch. And not everyone likes to cook. That's where the slow cooker comes in to help. Once you have the ingredients, all you need to do is a little chopping, then throw them in.

EASY PREP

I believe slow cooking should be easy. That's why you won't find a recipe in here with more than 15 minutes of prep time. If you do have some extra time, though, you can opt to brown your meat before adding it to the slow cooker.

Browning the meat will render the fat, which you can discard before proceeding with the recipe, and will also give the flavor another level of depth. Even lean meat has some fat, though if you use a lean-enough cut, searing it first is not necessary. Sautéing vegetables beforehand is also optional. But remember this: Searing and sautéing do add flavor to whatever you are cooking, which can be a big plus when you are on a diet. It might be worth the extra step.

EASY COOK

Slow cookers are perfect for low-carb recipes. I have one word for you: meat. The low-and-slow method makes even the toughest cuts of beef, pork, or lamb succulent and tender. If you're trying to incorporate more meatless meals into your low-carb eating plan, there are plenty of veggies in this cookbook, too. Regardless of what you're cooking, the slow cooker just makes life easier. With minimal prep, you'll have a delicious low-carb meal waiting for you. Sit back and let the slow cooker do most of the work.

A NOTE ON SWEETENER

In some recipes you'll see an ingredient called erythritol. Erythritol is a natural sugar alcohol (and common sugar replacement) found in certain fruits and fermented foods, like grapes, watermelon, and cheese. Containing 95 percent fewer calories and carbs than sugar, it's also not as sweet, so you can't use the same amount of erythritol as you would use of sugar. Approximately 1⅓ cups of erythritol is equal to 1 cup of sugar. Popular erythritol brands include Swerve, Truvia, and ZSweet. You can find these brands at most grocery stores or online.

Go-to Ingredients

Keeping a well-stocked pantry is the key to successful low-carb cooking. By having basic yet versatile ingredients always on hand, you'll be able to put together slow cooker recipes with ease. Here are my go-to ingredients for low-carb slow cooking, as well as some shopping and storage tips. You'll find these ingredients used in many of the recipes in this cookbook.

HERBS AND SPICES

Use dried herbs. Dried herbs will withstand the long cook times of a slow cooker better than delicate, fresh herbs. Their flavor is also more concentrated, so you can use them in smaller amounts. Plus, they last much longer than fresh—as long as 2 to 3 years when stored in a cool, dry place—whereas fresh herbs need to be used within a few days of purchase. If you prefer using fresh herbs, they should be added during the last hour of cook time. In these recipes, all herbs and spices are assumed to be dried or ground unless specifically noted as fresh.

- basil
- black pepper
- cayenne pepper
- chili powder
- cilantro (fresh)

- cumin
- garlic powder
- ginger (ground and fresh)
- oregano
- paprika

- parsley (dried and fresh)
- rosemary (dried and fresh)
- thyme (dried and fresh)
- salt

PANTRY

Look for salt-free or low-sodium canned goods at all times. Always check the label for added (meaning: unwanted) ingredients.

- broth and stock (store-bought)
- canned tomatoes

- coconut oil
- extra-virgin olive oil
- garlic (fresh)

- ghee (page 129)
- onions

When buying frozen vegetables, read the labels and make sure to choose products with no added ingredients. Frozen vegetables will last for months in your freezer.

- almond milk
- assorted cheeses
- broth and stock (homemade; see chapter 9)
- eggs
- fresh produce
- frozen vegetables
- half and half
- heavy (whipping) cream

Slow Cooker Considerations

The most important factor in choosing a slow cooker is size. Slow cookers come in a bunch of different sizes: under 2 quarts, 3.5 quarts; 4, 5, or 6 quarts; and 7 quarts or larger. If you're feeding only one or two people, you'll never need more than a 3.5-quart slow cooker. If you're feeding three to five people, you'll need one that is 4 to 6 quarts. Any more people than that, and you'll need a 7-quart slow cooker or larger, or you'll need to look into purchasing two. Almost all the recipes in this cookbook can be made in a 3.5-quart slow cooker.

The one thing you don't want to do is use a slow cooker that's too big for the amount of food you're cooking. If you don't have enough food to fill the slow cooker to at least 75 percent full, then you will risk burning the food. That shouldn't be a problem for any of the recipes in this book if you are using a 3.5-quart slow cooker.

Meal Planning

I like to meal plan because it allows me to eat healthy, control portions, and save time and money. Slow cookers were made for planning ahead. I don't know about you, but I don't want to stand in the kitchen all day prepping my meals for the week. Put your recipes in the slow cooker and let it do the work

MULTICOOKER MADNESS

Who has an Instant Pot? This appliance has become super popular because it can be used as both a pressure cooker and a slow cooker. You can make any of the recipes in this book using the Slow Cook function on the Instant Pot. Plus, there are several recipes in the book that can be prepared using the Pressure Cook (formerly Manual) setting, which is great if you don't have time to wait for dinner. I have two Instant Pots myself and, while I call myself the Fit Slow Cooker Queen, I find that I do use my Instant Pots at least once a week. And that's usually when I forget to put the food in the slow cooker on time! Having made the same recipes in both a slow cooker and an Instant Pot, trust me, they are delicious either way. To me, it's all about what is convenient to use that day. I've provided tips in the recipes so you can easily adapt them.

for you. You can cook meats and vegetables in bulk, either together or separately, and store them in the refrigerator or freezer to enjoy later in the week. All they will need is a quick heat-up, and they will be ready to eat.

SAMPLE MEAL PLAN

On the next page is an example of a weeklong meal plan that incorporates some of the low-carb slow cooker recipes in this book to help kick-start your weight-loss goals. Please take into consideration the difference between men and women when it comes to losing weight. Even though you can eat the same recipes, losing weight varies by sex and by your activity level, so you may need to adjust the size of the portions. For example, on average, a moderately active woman needs 2,000 calories a day; a male with a similar exercise pattern needs 2,800 calories.

This is a slow cooker cookbook, so all the recipes are cooked with a slow cooker, but I understand that using one to make every meal is not realistic. Heck, I don't even do that. The solution is leftovers. Have your leftover dinners for lunch, like I do. Note: The meal suggestions here include a mix of slow cooker recipes from this book and simple meals that don't really require a recipe (italicized).

	BREAKFAST	LUNCH	DINNER
Monday	Huevos Rancheros (page 24)	*Simple grilled salmon salad*	Chicken Saltimbocca (page 85)
Tuesday	*Eggs cooked in ghee with bell peppers, topped with avocado*	Chicken Saltimbocca leftovers	Jerk Pork Chops (page 102)
Wednesday	Huevos Rancheros leftovers	*Bunless hamburger with side salad*	Thai Shrimp Soup (page 65)
Thursday	*Greek yogurt with berries*	Thai Shrimp Soup leftovers	Beef Enchilada Casserole (page 92)
Friday	*Eggs cooked in ghee with a couple tablespoons of shredded cheese*	Beef Enchilada Casserole leftovers	Indian Cauliflower Bake (page 62)
Saturday	*Greek yogurt with berries*	*Grilled 4-ounce salmon fillet or chicken breast, Lemon-Garlic Asparagus (page 32)*	Pork Carnitas (page 104)
Sunday	Crustless Quiche Lorraine (page 25)	Pork Carnitas leftovers	Mediterranean-Stuffed Chicken Breasts (page 86)

Top Tips and Takeaways

While slow cooking in general is fairly easy, there are a few tips and tricks to keep in mind for maximum success:

Leave the lid on. Set it and forget it (unless the recipe instructs you to add an ingredient toward the end of the cooking time). Lifting the lid releases heat and just taking a quick peek can add as much as 30 minutes of additional cooking time!

Don't overcrowd the slow cooker. This will lead to the food cooking unevenly or not all the way through.

Chop the ingredients in large chunks, roughly the same size. This will allow them to cook evenly, and it will particularly help vegetables from falling apart when they get very soft.

Cut to fit. If your meat is too big, cut it into pieces. Do the same for vegetables.

Use frozen vegetables. They're less expensive than fresh, they are just as good nutritionally, and you can store them in your freezer so they'll last longer.

Trim the fat. Most meat will be falling-off-the-bone tender when it's done cooking, so the fat will be liquefied and almost impossible to remove after the fact. Save yourself the trouble and trim it off before adding meat to the slow cooker.

Set the timer and plan accordingly. Leaner proteins, like white-meat poultry, can overcook in a slow cooker, so mind the time. No one wants to eat dry, overcooked chicken.

Let's Get Cooking

This cookbook is a collection of classic recipes that I adjusted to be low-carb—and brand-new low-carb recipes I created for you to enjoy. While there is no official definition of a low-carb diet, most low-carb eating plans essentially mean eating 50 grams of carbohydrates or less a day, so I really tried to keep the carbs per serving in each recipe as low as possible without compromising on flavor and without being too extreme. Only two recipes in this book exceed 20 grams total carbs per serving.

It's important to me to make cooking as simple as possible for you, so every recipe can be prepped in 15 minutes or less. And that's leaving plenty of time for everything. I provide tips so you will better understand why certain ingredients are healthy and which ingredients make good substitutes. From low-carb stews and soups, to vegetarian and seafood recipes, to roasts and casseroles, there is something for everyone here. I think you'll find that you're pleasantly surprised with the high level of flavor the dishes have.

Are you ready to start low-carb slow cooking? Which recipe will you try first?

SLOW COOKER FOOD SAFETY

There are a few things you need to be aware of when it comes to slow cooking.

- Don't leave food in the slow cooker too long once it's done. It's okay to keep certain dishes on the Warm setting, but you should take cooked food out the slow cooker within a couple of hours. Otherwise you risk bacteria growth.

- Do not reheat leftover food in a slow cooker. Use the microwave or stove.

- Before serving, be sure to check the internal temperature of food to make sure it is safe to eat. Here are the guidelines for minimum safe temperatures:
  - » Steaks, roasts, chops: 145°F
  - » Ground meat: 160°F
  - » Eggs: 160°F
  - » Poultry: 165°F
  - » Soups, stews, and sauces: 165°F

Granola, page 18

breakfast & brunch

Asparagus Cauliflower Hash

Serves 8 / **Prep time:** 10 minutes / **Cook time:** 6 to 8 hours on low / 3 to 4 hours on high

Asparagus is loaded with nutrients, and it is a very good source of fiber and vitamins A and C. It's a great vegetable to choose if you're watching your blood sugar. Cauliflower has become a popular low-carb replacement for rice or potatoes. Use it here to make hash browns; paired with the cheese and eggs, you won't be able to tell it's not potatoes.

Cooking spray

12 large eggs

½ cup low-fat 1% milk

2 cups shredded part-skim mozzarella cheese

1 teaspoon salt

¼ teaspoon freshly ground black pepper

1 medium head cauliflower, shredded or riced

1 pound asparagus, chopped

1. Coat a slow cooker generously with cooking spray.

2. In a large bowl, whisk together the eggs, milk, cheese, salt, and pepper.

3. Add half the cauliflower to the bottom of the slow cooker. Top with half the asparagus. Repeat with the remaining cauliflower and asparagus.

4. Pour the eggs into the slow cooker.

5. Cook on low for 6 to 8 hours or on high for 3 to 4 hours, or until eggs are set.

Ingredient tip: If asparagus isn't your favorite vegetable, feel free to use a preferred slow cooker–friendly vegetable, like mushrooms or broccoli.

PER SERVING: Calories: 209; Fat: 12g; Carbohydrates: 9g; Fiber: 3g; Protein: 18g; Sodium: 574mg

Broccoli, Bacon, and Cheese Quiche

Serves 8 / **Prep time:** 5 minutes / **Cook time:** 6 to 8 hours on low / 3 to 4 hours on high

A quiche without the crust? There's no denying the appeal of the deliciously buttery and flaky quiche crust, but there is so much flavor in this recipe that I promise you won't miss it ... too much. If you're vegetarian, omit the bacon and load this up with your favorite additional vegetables. Some of mine include zucchini, onions, and mushrooms.

Cooking spray

8 large eggs

2 cups reduced-fat 2% milk

½ cup grated Parmesan cheese

½ teaspoon salt

2 pounds frozen broccoli florets, thawed

6 ounces bacon, cooked and crumbled

¾ cup shredded medium Cheddar cheese, divided

1. Coat a slow cooker generously with cooking spray.

2. In a medium bowl, whisk together the eggs, milk, Parmesan, and salt.

3. Add the broccoli, bacon, and half the Cheddar cheese to the slow cooker. Pour in the egg mixture. Top with the remaining Cheddar cheese.

4. Cook on low for 6 to 8 hours or on high for 3 to 4 hours, or until the eggs are set.

Ingredient tip: Fresh broccoli can be used in place of frozen.

Substitution tip: Try this with chopped asparagus instead of broccoli.

PER SERVING: Calories: 363; Fat: 24g; Carbohydrates: 17g; Fiber: 7g; Protein: 25g; Sodium: 648mg

Granola

Serves 8 / **Prep time:** 10 minutes / **Cook time:** 6 hours on low / 3 hours on high

When you think low-carb, granola usually isn't at the top of the list. And most people think store-bought granola is healthy, so they don't make their own. Unfortunately, a lot of store-bought granola is covered in—guess what?—sugar. Lucky for you, this low-carb version is really easy to make (and it tastes great), and you get to be in control of the ingredients, ensuring they are natural with no added fillers.

Cooking spray

2½ cups almonds

¼ cup unsweetened coconut flakes

½ cup dried berries

¼ cup chia seeds

1 teaspoon cinnamon

½ teaspoon salt

¼ teaspoon nutmeg

¼ cup coconut oil

1 teaspoon vanilla

1. Coat the sides of a slow cooker generously with cooking spray.

2. Add the almonds, coconut flakes, dried berries, chia seeds, cinnamon, salt, and nutmeg to the slow cooker.

3. In a medium bowl, melt the coconut oil. Whisk in the vanilla.

4. Pour the mixture into the slow cooker, stirring to make sure all the ingredients are moistened.

5. Lay a small towel or 2 paper towels in between the slow cooker and the lid to create a barrier. This will prevent the condensation from dripping on the granola while it cooks. It's important to catch the condensation or you will end up with soggy granola.

6. Cook mixture on low for 6 hours or on high for 3 hours.

7. Transfer the granola to a baking sheet to cool.

Ingredient tip: Strawberries, blueberries, or raspberries are great choices for this recipe because of their lower carb amounts.

Make-ahead tip: You can store the granola in an airtight container in the refrigerator for up to 2 weeks or freeze it for up to 2 months. Defrost in the refrigerator before serving.

PER SERVING: Calories: 338; Fat: 27g; Carbohydrates: 19g; Fiber: 7g; Protein: 9g; Sodium: 295mg

Sausage and Egg Scramble

Serves 8 / **Prep time:** 5 minutes / **Cook time:** 6 to 8 hours on low / 3 to 4 hours on high

With lots of sausage and cheese, this hearty breakfast will keep you going until lunch-time. I like to use low-fat, mild ground pork sausage, but you could also try turkey sausage or vegetarian sausage.

Cooking spray

8 ounces low-fat ground pork sausage

12 large eggs

1 pound low-fat Cheddar cheese, shredded

½ cup almond milk

½ teaspoon salt

¼ teaspoon freshly ground black pepper

1. Coat a slow cooker generously with cooking spray.

2. Add sausage, eggs, cheese, almond milk, salt, and pepper to the slow cooker. Stir to mix well.

3. Cook on low for 6 to 8 hours or on high for 3 to 4 hours, or until the eggs are set.

4. Use a fork to "scramble" the mixture before serving.

Make-ahead tip: This recipe is great to make the night before. Load up the ingredients and press the On button right before you go to bed, and you'll wake up to a delicious, savory breakfast.

Make it keto: To increase the fat content to a more keto-friendly level, substitute heavy (whipping) cream in place of the almond milk.

PER SERVING: Calories: 208; Fat: 11g; Carbohydrates: 2g; Fiber: 0g; Protein: 23g; Sodium: 687mg

Tomato and Feta Frittata

Serves 8 / **Prep time:** 5 minutes / **Cook time:** 6 to 8 hours on low / 3 to 4 hours on high

A frittata is an egg-based Italian dish similar to an omelet or a crustless quiche. For this version I like to use Roma tomatoes, though the recipe is very flexible and you can use whatever tomato suits your fancy. If you're a feta fan, go ahead and bump up the quantity to 6 ounces.

Cooking spray

12 large eggs

1½ cups chopped fresh tomatoes

4 ounces feta cheese, crumbled

½ cup half and half

1 garlic clove, minced

1 teaspoon dried chopped onion

½ teaspoon dried basil

½ teaspoon salt

¼ teaspoon freshly ground black pepper

1. Coat a slow cooker generously with cooking spray.
2. In a medium bowl, whisk together the eggs, tomatoes, feta, half and half, garlic, onion, basil, salt, and pepper.
3. Pour the mixture into the slow cooker.
4. Cook on low for 6 to 8 hours or on high for 3 to 4 hours, or until the eggs are set.

Substitution tip: Lighten up this frittata by using egg whites. Two cups of egg whites are the approximate equivalent to 12 eggs.

Make it Whole30: Don't use the feta cheese.

PER SERVING: Calories: 171; Fat: 12g; Carbohydrates: 4g; Fiber: 1g; Protein: 12g; Sodium: 320mg

Tex-Mex Egg Scramble

Serves 8 / **Prep time:** 10 minutes / **Cook time:** 6 to 8 hours on low / 3 to 4 hours on high

Migas is a Tex-Mex breakfast dish consisting of strips of fried tortillas mixed into scrambled eggs, cheese, and salsa. This is my low-carb ode to that Latin-inspired dish. I've omitted the tortillas, but if you can find a low-carb tortilla that fits your lifestyle, then by all means, sneak one in.

Cooking spray

12 large eggs

⅓ cup reduced-fat 2% milk

4 ounces Cheddar cheese, shredded

1 teaspoon salt

½ teaspoon freshly ground black pepper

1 small onion, chopped

2 bell peppers, seeded and chopped

1 jalapeño, seeded and chopped

¼ cup cherry tomatoes, sliced

⅓ cup chopped fresh cilantro

1. Coat a slow cooker generously with cooking spray.
2. In a medium bowl, whisk together the eggs, milk, cheese, salt, black pepper, onion, bell peppers, jalapeño, tomatoes, and cilantro.
3. Pour the mixture into the slow cooker.
4. Cook on low for 6 to 8 hours or on high for 3 to 4 hours, or until the eggs are set.
5. Use a fork to "scramble" the mixture before serving.

Make it paleo: Omit the cheese. There isn't very much cheese in this recipe, so you probably won't miss it anyway.

PER SERVING: Calories: 188; Fat: 12g; Carbohydrates: 5g; Fiber: 1g; Protein: 14g; Sodium: 497mg

Cheesy Egg-Stuffed Bell Peppers

Serves 4 / **Prep time:** 5 minutes / **Cook time:** 4 to 6 hours on low / 2 to 3 hours on high

This is a basic recipe that can be jazzed up by adding your favorite chopped vegetables or cooked meats. It is also pretty enough to serve at your next home-cooked brunch.

4 bell peppers

4 large eggs

8 ounces Cheddar cheese, shredded

½ teaspoon salt

¼ teaspoon freshly ground black pepper

1. Cut the tops off the bell peppers and clean out the ribs and seeds. Place into a slow cooker.

2. In a small bowl, whisk together the eggs, cheese, salt, and pepper.

3. Pour ¼ of the egg mixture into each pepper.

4. Cook on low for 4 to 6 hours or on high for 2 to 3 hours, or until the eggs are fully set.

Ingredient tip: Jazz this recipe up a bit with more veggies and/or meat (add them to the peppers when you add the eggs). Make this with green, yellow, or red bell peppers (or a combination). Or add ½ cup crumbled bacon in the egg mixture.

Make it keto: Add ¼ teaspoon Ghee (page 129) to the top of each bell pepper before cooking.

PER SERVING: Calories: 176; Fat: 12g; Carbohydrates: 6g; Fiber: 2g; Protein: 11g; Sodium: 370mg

Cauliflower Cheese "Grits"

Serves 4 / **Prep time:** 10 minutes / **Cook time:** 6 to 8 hours on low / 3 to 4 hours on high

Grits taste so great but they don't make the cut when it comes to carbs. Enter cauliflower. Not only is this versatile veggie low-carb, but it has fewer calories and more fiber. And the flavor will make you forget about those grits. It's easy to play around with the consistency here—less water for thicker grits, more water if you like your grits thinner.

4 cups riced or grated cauliflower (about 1 head)

¾ cup water

¼ cup shredded Cheddar cheese

2 teaspoons butter

¼ teaspoon salt

⅛ teaspoon freshly ground black pepper

1. Add the cauliflower, water, cheese, butter, salt, and pepper to a slow cooker. Stir to mix well.

2. Cook on low for 6 to 8 hours or on high for 3 to 4 hours.

Ingredient tip: If ricing or grating the cauliflower yourself, do not use frozen or previously frozen cauliflower. Only fresh will work.

Make it faster: Cook this in an Instant Pot. Add all the ingredients, stir to mix well, and cook on Manual for 7 minutes. Use a quick release.

PER SERVING: Calories: 84; Fat: 5g; Carbohydrates: 8g; Fiber: 3g; Protein: 5g; Sodium: 253mg

Huevos Rancheros

Serves 6 / **Prep time:** 10 minutes / **Cook time:** 4 to 6 hours on low / 2 to 3 hours on high

This Mexican-flavored one-pot dish is ideal for breakfast or brunch. Huevos Rancheros are usually served over fried tortillas, but I've eliminated those here, choosing instead to emphasize the cheese, chorizo, tomatoes, and cumin, which form the classic flavors of this dish. Since the eggs are poached, you will need to serve this immediately rather than leave it on the warm setting.

Cooking spray

1 (28-ounce) can low-sodium or no-salt-added diced tomatoes

8 ounces low-sodium or no-salt-added tomato sauce

2 tablespoons extra-virgin olive oil

4 ounces chorizo, cooked and crumbled

1 small onion, chopped

1 red bell pepper, seeded and diced

1 tablespoon cumin

½ teaspoon paprika

½ teaspoon salt

¼ teaspoon freshly ground black pepper

1½ cups shredded Cheddar cheese

6 large eggs

1. Coat a slow cooker generously with cooking spray.

2. Add the diced tomatoes, tomato sauce, olive oil, chorizo, onion, bell pepper, cumin, paprika, salt, black pepper, and cheese to the slow cooker. Stir to mix well.

3. Cook on low for 4 to 6 hours or on high for 2 to 3 hours.

4. Using a spoon, dig 6 small wells in the sauce. Crack one egg into each well.

5. Cover and cook on high for an additional 10 to 20 minutes. Serve immediately.

Make it Whole30: Simply omit the cheese.

PER SERVING: Calories: 270; Fat: 20g; Carbohydrates: 9g; Fiber: 3g; Protein: 15g; Sodium: 632mg

Crustless Quiche Lorraine

Serves 6 / **Prep time:** 10 minutes / **Cook time:** 4 to 6 hours on low / 2 to 3 hours on high

This classic easily goes low-carb by getting rid of the crust, which you will not miss because the flavor comes from the bacon, eggs, and cheese. Serve for an Easter brunch or any other gathering that you'd like to be a little extra special.

Cooking spray

5 large eggs

5 egg whites

8 ounces bacon, cooked and crumbled

½ cup chopped onion

1 tablespoon extra-virgin olive oil

1 cup reduced-fat 2% milk

1 cup shredded Swiss cheese

½ teaspoon salt

½ teaspoon freshly ground black pepper

½ teaspoon chives

1. Coat a slow cooker generously with cooking spray.

2. In a large bowl, whisk together the eggs, egg whites, bacon, onion, olive oil, milk, cheese, salt, pepper, and chives. Pour into the slow cooker.

3. Cook on low for 4 to 6 hours or on high for 2 to 3 hours.

Make it keto: Substitute half and half or heavy (whipping) cream for the milk.

Substitution tip: Use 8 ounces cooked and chopped ham instead of bacon.

PER SERVING: Calories: 271; Fat: 16g; Carbohydrates: 4g; Fiber: 0g; Protein: 26g; Sodium: 376mg

Three-Cheese Omelet

Serves 8 / **Prep time:** 5 minutes / **Cook time:** 6 to 8 hours on low / 3 to 4 hours on high

Where are my cheese lovers? This one is for you. This is another recipe that can be personalized with your favorite chopped veggies and cooked meats, but with three cheeses, it's just about perfect on its own.

Cooking spray

8 large eggs

½ cup low-fat 1% milk

1 pound low-fat cheese (choose a combination of three: Cheddar, Jack, Colby, Swiss, or your favorite), shredded

½ teaspoon salt

¼ teaspoon freshly ground black pepper

1. Coat a slow cooker generously with cooking spray.

2. In a medium bowl, whisk together the eggs, milk, cheese, salt, and pepper. Pour into the slow cooker.

3. Cook on low for 6 to 8 hours or on high for 3 to 4 hours, or until the eggs are set.

Ingredient tip: For a different flavor, substitute a soft cheese, like burrata or mozzarella.

Make it faster: Use your Instant Pot. Coat a large ramekin with cooking spray and pour in the omelet mixture. Add 1 cup of water to the Instant Pot, place the ramekin inside, and secure the lid. Select Manual and pressure cook for 10 minutes. Use the natural release or the quick release.

PER SERVING: Calories: 176; Fat: 9g; Carbohydrates: 2g; Fiber: 0g; Protein: 21g; Sodium: 716mg

Avocado and Egg Casserole

Serves 8 / **Prep time:** 5 minutes / **Cook time:** 6 to 8 hours on low / 3 to 4 hours on high

The good fats in avocado make this recipe keto-friendly and give the finished dish a creamy texture. Even though the avocado is cooked with the eggs in the slow cooker, the result is a cheesy omelet that tastes like guacamole.

Cooking spray

8 large eggs

1 avocado, sliced

1½ cups shredded low-fat Cheddar cheese

½ cup low-fat 1% milk

½ teaspoon salt

¼ teaspoon freshly ground black pepper

1. Coat a slow cooker with cooking spray.

2. In a medium bowl, whisk together the eggs, avocado, cheese, milk, salt, and pepper. Pour into the slow cooker.

3. Cook on low for 6 to 8 hours or on high for 3 to 4 hours.

Ingredient tip: You can turn this into a scramble by using a fork to "scramble" the casserole before serving.

PER SERVING: Calories: 155; Fat: 10g; Carbohydrates: 4g; Fiber: 2g; Protein: 13g; Sodium: 410mg

Garlic-Parmesan Green Beans, page 36

vegetables & sides

Cauliflower Mac and Cheese

Serves 6 / **Prep time:** 10 minutes / **Cook time:** 4 to 6 hours on low / 2 to 3 hours on high

Macaroni and cheese lovers rejoice! When you swap out the pasta and use cauliflower, you're left with a low-carb taste sensation that is creamy and filling. It makes great leftovers and the kids will like it, too. If the sauce seems too thick after it's finished cooking, stir in a little water or vegetable broth.

Cooking spray

2 medium heads cauliflower, cut into small florets

1 small onion, diced

3 cups Cheese Sauce (page 126)

1. Coat a slow cooker generously with cooking spray.
2. Add the cauliflower and onion to the slow cooker.
3. Pour the cheese sauce over the top.
4. Cook on low for 4 to 6 hours or on high for 2 to 3 hours, or until the cauliflower is tender.

Ingredient tip: There are lots of ways to vary the flavors of this dish. Try adding crumbled bacon or chopped ham. How about chopped asparagus or broccoli?

PER SERVING: Calories: 246; Fat: 15g; Carbohydrates: 15g; Fiber: 4g; Protein: 16g; Sodium: 361mg

Try: Sauce milk-free mac & cheese sauce

1 C butter
6 TBS shallots
3 C red or yellow pots
3/4 c carrots
1 C onion
3 C H₂0
3/4 C raw cashews
3 tsp salt
3/4 tsp garlic

3/4 tsp Dijon
3 TBS lemon juice
3/4 tsp black pepper
3/8 tsp cayenne
3/4 tsp paprika

Balsamic and Bacon Vegetable Medley

Serves 4 / **Prep time:** 15 minutes / **Cook time:** 4 to 6 hours on low / 2 to 3 hours on high

Here is a side dish perfect for summer, when these vegetables will be at their freshest and most flavorful. By cooking in a slow cooker, you don't need to stand over a hot stove. Feel free to swap in whatever veggies you like the best. And it's never wrong to add a little extra bacon.

Cooking spray

8 ounces bacon, cooked and crumbled

1 small onion, chopped

2 bell peppers, seeded and chopped

3 ounces carrots, peeled and chopped

3 ounces green beans, cut into 1-inch pieces

3 ounces Brussels sprouts, trimmed and halved

3 ounces beets, peeled and chopped

3 ounces summer squash or zucchini, chopped

¼ cup water

1 tablespoon extra-virgin olive oil

2 tablespoons balsamic vinegar

1. Coat a slow cooker generously with cooking spray.

2. Add the bacon, onion, bell peppers, carrots, green beans, Brussels sprouts, beets, and squash to the slow cooker.

3. In a small bowl, mix together the water, olive oil, and vinegar to make a sauce. Pour it over the top of the vegetables.

4. Cook on low for 4 to 6 hours or on high for 2 to 3 hours, or until Brussels sprouts are tender.

Ingredient tip: Make this cheesy and sprinkle ¼ cup of crumbled feta or blue cheese over the top after cooking.

PER SERVING: Calories: 133; Fat: 6g; Carbohydrates: 18g; Fiber: 6g; Protein: 5g; Sodium: 82mg

Lemon-Garlic Asparagus

Serves 4 / **Prep time:** 10 minutes / **Cook time:** 4 to 6 hours on low / 2 to 3 hours on high

Make this recipe your go-to holiday side dish. The lemon-garlic sauce turns a simple vegetable dish into something special enough to make whenever you want to entertain. And you'll still be sticking to your diet!

2 pounds asparagus, ends trimmed

Juice of 2 lemons (4 to 6 tablespoons)

½ cup low-sodium chicken broth or water

2 garlic cloves, minced

1 teaspoon basil

1 teaspoon garlic salt

½ teaspoon freshly ground black pepper

¼ teaspoon red pepper flakes

1 lemon, sliced

1. Place the asparagus in the bottom of the slow cooker.
2. In a small bowl, mix together the lemon juice, broth, garlic, basil, garlic salt, black pepper, and red pepper flakes.
3. Pour the sauce over the asparagus, then top with the lemon slices.
4. Cook on low for 4 to 6 hours or on high for 2 to 3 hours.

Ingredient tip: The asparagus will lose some of its vibrant green color as it cooks, but it will taste just as delicious, I promise.

PER SERVING: Calories: 66; Fat: 1g; Carbohydrates: 14g; Fiber: 6g; Protein: 6g; Sodium: 505mg

Brussels Sprouts au Gratin

Serves 8 / **Prep time:** 15 minutes / **Cook time:** 6 to 8 hours on low / 3 to 4 hours on high

I love Brussels sprouts but I know not everyone does, so I created a creamy cheese sauce to pour over them. Not only is this dish absolutely delicious, but you'll rest easy knowing that it's still low in carbs. If you happen to have some Cheese Sauce (page 126) in the refrigerator, you can use that instead of the sauce ingredients here.

Cooking spray

2 pounds Brussels sprouts, trimmed and halved

¼ cup butter, melted

2 tablespoons cornstarch

¼ cup chopped onion

1 cup half and half

2 cups shredded Gruyère cheese

1. Coat a slow cooker generously with cooking spray.

2. Add the Brussels sprouts to the slow cooker.

3. In a medium bowl, mix together the butter, cornstarch, onion, half and half, and cheese until well blended. Pour the mixture over the vegetables.

4. Cook on low for 6 to 8 hours or on high for 3 to 4 hours.

Make it keto: Substitute Ghee (page 129) for the butter and add 8 ounces cooked, crumbled bacon.

PER SERVING: Calories: 257; Fat: 18g; Carbohydrates: 14g; Fiber: 4g; Protein: 13g; Sodium: 286mg

Herbed Spaghetti Squash Casserole

Serves 6 / **Prep time:** 15 minutes / **Cook time:** 4 to 6 hours on low / 2 to 3 hours on high

Simple herbs from your pantry spice up this easy spaghetti squash casserole. This is a nice dish to bring to a potluck or family reunion. Everyone will like it and most people won't realize that you are actually sticking to a low-carb diet.

1 (2-pound) spaghetti squash

Cooking spray

1 cup low-sodium or no-salt-added diced tomatoes

¼ teaspoon oregano

¼ teaspoon rosemary

¼ teaspoon thyme

¼ teaspoon parsley

¼ teaspoon basil

½ teaspoon salt

¼ teaspoon freshly ground black pepper

4 ounces mozzarella cheese, shredded

⅓ cup grated Parmesan cheese

¼ cup water

1. Pierce the spaghetti squash all over with a knife, place in a microwave-safe dish, and microwave for 7 to 10 minutes or until soft. Be careful removing the squash from the microwave because it will be very hot.

2. Cut the squash in half and scoop out and discard the seeds.

3. Use a fork to scrape out the spaghetti-like strands into a large bowl.

4. Coat a slow cooker generously with cooking spray.

5. Add the spaghetti squash strands, tomatoes, oregano, rosemary, thyme, parsley, basil, salt, pepper, mozzarella, Parmesan, and water to the slow cooker. Stir to mix well.

6. Cook on low for 4 to 6 hours or on high for 2 to 3 hours.

Ingredient tip: Spaghetti squash will release water when cooked. To reduce that amount of liquid, place the spaghetti squash strands on a couple paper towels, sprinkle with ½ teaspoon of salt, and let them sit for about 5 minutes. Wring the excess water out before adding them back the slow cooker.

PER SERVING: Calories: 142; Fat: 6g; Carbohydrates: 15g; Fiber: 3g; Protein: 8g; Sodium: 474mg

Tomatoes with Kale and Feta

Serves 6 / **Prep time:** 10 minutes / **Cook time:** 4 to 6 hours on low / 2 to 3 hours on high

Make this recipe when it's tomato season and fresh, ripe tomatoes are plentiful at the market. I keep this dish as simple as possible to let the tomatoes shine.

Cooking spray

1 cup chopped kale

3 pounds tomatoes, sliced

¼ cup balsamic vinegar

1 tablespoon extra-virgin olive oil

½ teaspoon salt

¼ teaspoon freshly ground black pepper

1 cup crumbled feta cheese

1. Coat a slow cooker generously with cooking spray.

2. Place the kale in the bottom of the slow cooker. Top with the tomato slices.

3. In a small bowl, mix together the balsamic vinegar, olive oil, salt, and pepper. Pour the mixture over the top of the kale and tomatoes.

4. Cook on low for 4 to 6 hours or on high for 2 to 3 hours.

5. Top with the crumbled feta and serve.

Make it paleo or Whole30: Omit the cheese.

PER SERVING: Calories: 138; Fat: 8g; Carbohydrates: 12g; Fiber: 3g; Protein: 6g; Sodium: 438mg

Garlic-Parmesan Green Beans

Serves 6 / **Prep time:** 10 minutes / **Cook time:** 4 to 6 hours on low / 2 to 3 hours on high

When you cook the green beans, broth, butter, garlic, and cheese, your kitchen will be filled with incredible aromas. The slow cooker will look pretty full when this starts cooking, but the ingredients will cook down as the hours go by.

3 pounds green beans, trimmed

⅓ cup low-sodium chicken broth

4 garlic cloves, minced

⅔ cup shaved Parmesan cheese

½ teaspoon salt

¼ teaspoon freshly ground black pepper

1 tablespoon unsalted butter, cut into small pieces

1. Place the green beans into a slow cooker.
2. Pour the broth over the top. Sprinkle the garlic, Parmesan, salt, and pepper over the top.
3. Top with the pieces of butter.
4. Cook on low for 4 to 6 hours or on high for 2 to 3 hours.

Make it keto: Use Ghee (page 129) instead of butter, and sprinkle more Parmesan on top prior to serving.

PER SERVING: Calories: 148; Fat: 6g; Carbohydrates: 17g; Fiber: 6g; Protein: 10g; Sodium: 438mg

Easy Cheesy Ratatouille

Serves 8 / **Prep time:** 15 minutes / **Cook time:** 4 to 6 hours on low / 2 to 3 hours on high

There are a lot of variations of ratatouille recipes out in the world because of the wide variety of vegetables that work well together. I've opted to stick with basic, common ingredients so you'll be able to find them easily in the store, but feel free to swap in other veggies where you feel like it.

1 pound eggplant, peeled and chopped

1 cup grated Parmesan cheese

1 large onion, chopped

1 medium zucchini, chopped

1 bell pepper, seeded and chopped

1 (28-ounce) can low-sodium or no-salt-added diced tomatoes

2 garlic cloves, minced

1 tablespoon extra-virgin olive oil

½ teaspoon salt

½ teaspoon tarragon

½ teaspoon rosemary

½ teaspoon thyme

½ teaspoon basil

1. Add the eggplant, cheese, onion, zucchini, bell pepper, tomatoes, garlic, olive oil, salt, tarragon, rosemary, thyme, and basil to the slow cooker. Stir to mix well.

2. Cook on low for 4 to 6 hours or on high for 2 to 3 hours.

Make it faster: Add all the ingredients to your Instant Pot and mix together. Cook on Manual for 5 minutes and release the pressure naturally.

PER SERVING: Calories: 147; Fat: 5g; Carbohydrates: 18g; Fiber: 5g; Protein: 9g; Sodium: 485mg

Cauliflower "Pasta" Alfredo

Serves 10 / **Prep time:** 15 minutes / **Cook time:** 4 to 6 hours on low / 2 to 3 hours on high

Cauliflower replaces pasta here, resulting in a mouthwatering low-carb version of an Italian classic. These vegetables go quite well together, but you can easily substitute others, depending on what you find at the store.

3 cups chopped cauliflower

3 cups Alfredo Sauce (page 124)

1 cup Vegetable Broth (page 120) or store-bought low-sodium vegetable broth

1 cup heavy (whipping) cream

8 ounces mushrooms, sliced

8 ounces zucchini, sliced

1 onion, chopped

2 garlic cloves, minced

½ teaspoon salt

1 teaspoon basil

1 teaspoon parsley

1 cup shredded part-skim mozzarella cheese

1. Add all the cauliflower, alfredo sauce, broth, cream, mushrooms, zucchini, onion, garlic, salt, basil, parsley, and cheese to the slow cooker. Stir to mix well.

2. Cook on low for 4 to 6 hours or on high for 2 to 3 hours.

Ingredient tip: Stir in 1 cup of your favorite cooked meat, like ground sausage or ground beef, along with the other ingredients at the beginning of cook time. Or try adding 1 or 2 cups of chopped kale or spinach.

Substitution tip: Use yellow squash instead of zucchini.

PER SERVING: Calories: 373; Fat: 11g; Carbohydrates: 8g; Fiber: 2g; Protein: 11g; Sodium: 586mg

Herbed Portobello Mushrooms

Serves 4 / **Prep time:** 5 minutes / **Cook time:** 4 to 6 hours on low / 2 to 3 hours on high

Portobello mushrooms have a sturdy texture and a satisfying savory flavor that are reminiscent of meat, so they often stand in as a meat replacement for vegetarians. Here, they are cut into slices and cooked until tender, making this a very tasty side dish.

4 large portobello mushrooms, gills scooped out, sliced

1 small onion, sliced

2 teaspoons rosemary

½ teaspoon salt

⅛ teaspoon freshly ground black pepper

⅓ cup Vegetable Broth (page 120) or store-bought low-sodium vegetable broth

2 tablespoons unsalted butter, cut into pieces

1. Add the mushrooms, onion, rosemary, salt, and pepper to the slow cooker. Pour the broth on top.

2. Drop the pieces of butter over the top.

3. Cook on low for 4 to 6 hours or on high for 2 to 3 hours.

Substitution tip: Try eliminating the rosemary and using oregano, thyme, or sage (or a mixture of all of them).

PER SERVING: Calories: 81; Fat: 6g; Carbohydrates: 6g; Fiber: 2g; Protein: 2g; Sodium: 311mg

Spinach Pie

Serves 6 / **Prep time:** 10 minutes / **Cook time:** 6 to 8 hours on low / 3 to 4 hours on high

This crustless spinach pie is an easy quiche- or casserole-type dish that can be eaten for breakfast, lunch, or even dinner.

Cooking spray

1 bunch fresh spinach, chopped, or 1 (10-ounce) package frozen spinach (see Ingredient tip)

1 tablespoon extra-virgin olive oil

1 small onion, chopped

½ teaspoon salt

¼ teaspoon freshly ground black pepper

¼ teaspoon nutmeg

8 ounces part-skim mozzarella cheese, shredded

15 ounces part-skim ricotta cheese

½ cup grated Parmesan cheese

3 eggs, beaten

1. Coat a slow cooker generously with cooking spray.

2. In a medium bowl, mix together the spinach, olive oil, onion, salt, pepper, nutmeg, mozzarella, ricotta, Parmesan, and eggs.

3. Pour the mixture into the slow cooker.

4. Cook on low for 6 for 8 hours or on high for 3 to 4 hours.

Ingredient tip: If using frozen spinach, thaw first and squeeze out as much water as possible.

PER SERVING: Calories: 311; Fat: 20g; Carbohydrates: 9g; Fiber: 2g; Protein: 25g; Sodium: 709mg

Vegetarian Stuffed Peppers

Serves 4 / **Prep time:** 10 minutes / **Cook time:** 4 to 6 hours on low / 2 to 3 hours on high

This recipe requires a 6-quart slow cooker to make 4 servings. I've always loved stuffed peppers but they usually contain rice. I've swapped that out for cauliflower rice and it tastes so good.

Cooking spray

¼ cup water

¾ cup riced cauliflower

1 (15-ounce) can low-sodium crushed tomatoes

1 garlic clove, minced

¼ cup grated Parmesan cheese

1 tablespoon oregano

1 teaspoon basil

½ teaspoon salt

½ teaspoon freshly ground black pepper

4 bell peppers

1. Coat a slow cooker generously with cooking spray.
2. Pour the water into the slow cooker.
3. In a large bowl, mix together the cauliflower, tomatoes, garlic, Parmesan, oregano, basil, salt, and pepper.
4. Cut off the tops of the peppers and clean out the ribs and seeds.
5. Spoon ¼ of the filling into each pepper cavity.
6. Place the bell peppers in the slow cooker.
7. Cook on low for 4 to 6 hours or on high for 2 to 3 hours.

Make it paleo or Whole30: Omit the cheese.

Ingredient tip: Use yellow, red, or orange bell peppers. They have a milder flavor than green bell peppers. Add 1 cup chopped zucchini or eggplant to add a little more substance.

Substitution tip: If your slow cooker is smaller than 6 quarts, cut the recipe in half and make 2 stuffed peppers instead.

PER SERVING: Calories: 121; Fat: 2g; Carbohydrates: 19g; Fiber: 5g; Protein: 7g; Sodium: 557mg

Chicken Avocado Soup, page 48

soups, stews & chili

Garden Vegetable Soup

Serves 4 / **Prep time:** 10 minutes / **Cook time:** 6 to 8 hours on low / 3 to 4 hours on high

Grab your favorite vegetables for this super easy soup that is friendly for almost any healthy eating lifestyle: paleo, Whole30, vegetarian, vegan—it's a real diet pleaser. I love the combination of vegetables I've included below, but don't let that fence you in. Swap in whatever you find in the store that's fresh and low-carb. Try yellow squash instead of zucchini, or asparagus instead of green beans. Choose sturdy vegetables that won't turn to mush during the long cook time.

4 cups Vegetable Broth (page 120) or store-bought low-sodium vegetable broth

1 (15-ounce) can low-sodium or no-salt-added diced tomatoes

2 small zucchini, diced

2 carrots, peeled and chopped

4 ounces green beans, chopped

4 ounces kale, chopped

1 onion, diced

1 bell pepper, seeded and diced

2 garlic cloves, minced

1 tablespoon Italian seasoning

½ teaspoon salt

¼ teaspoon freshly ground black pepper

1 bay leaf

1. Add the broth, tomatoes, zucchini, carrots, green beans, kale, onion, bell pepper, garlic, Italian seasoning, salt, black pepper, and bay leaf to a slow cooker.

2. Cook on low for 6 to 8 hours or on high for 3 to 4 hours, or until vegetables are soft.

3. Remove the bay leaf prior to serving.

Make-ahead tip: Freezer meal: Divide the soup into 1-serving-size covered containers or in zip-top plastic bags and freeze for up to 3 months. In the morning, grab a container and bring it to the office for lunch.

PER SERVING: Calories: 141; Fat: 1g; Carbohydrates: 28g; Fiber: 8g; Protein: 7g; Sodium: 633mg

French Onion Soup

Serves 4 / Prep time: 10 minutes / **Cook time:** 6 to 8 hours on low / 3 to 4 hours on high

French onion soup is an all-time favorite of mine. I've never really been a big bread person, so this low-carb version is right up my alley. If you sauté the onions in a little butter on medium-low for about 10 minutes, your soup will have a richer, deeper flavor, so if you have the time, do that. But if you don't, never fear—it will still taste terrific. Slice the onions as thin as you can; if you have a mandoline, this is a good time to use it.

4 cups low-sodium beef broth

4 medium white onions, sliced as thin as possible

2 tablespoons unsalted butter

2 garlic cloves, minced

½ teaspoon salt

¼ teaspoon freshly ground black pepper

1 bay leaf

4 (1-ounce) slices provolone cheese

1. Add the broth, onions, butter, garlic, salt, pepper, and bay leaf to a slow cooker. Stir to mix well.

2. Cook on low for 6 to 8 hours or on high for 3 to 4 hours.

3. Preheat the oven to broil.

4. Ladle the soup into 4 oven-safe soup bowls and place on a baking sheet. Place 1 slice of provolone over the soup in each bowl, and broil for 1 minute, or until the cheese melts.

Ingredient tip: Instead of broiling the cheese, you can add it directly on top of the soup in the slow cooker about 10 minutes before the end of the cook time.

PER SERVING: Calories: 189; Fat: 11g; Carbohydrates: 13g; Fiber: 2g; Protein: 11g; Sodium: 601mg

Chicken Zoodle Soup

Serves 4 / **Prep time:** 10 minutes / **Cook time:** 4 to 6 hours on low / 2 to 3 hours on high

Zucchini noodles, or "zoodles," drastically reduce the carbs in this soup, and you can find zucchini at the store all year long. A spiralizer is a great kitchen gadget to have on hand to create perfectly uniform strands of zucchini in a flash. I recommend using chicken thighs because of their superior flavor; buy skinless if you can find them, or remove the skin yourself. This is another paleo- and Whole30-compliant recipe.

1 pound boneless, skinless chicken thighs

6 cups low-sodium chicken broth

2 medium zucchini, cut into spaghetti-like strands

2 celery stalks, sliced

2 carrots, peeled and chopped

2 garlic cloves, minced

1 teaspoon cumin

½ teaspoon salt

¼ teaspoon freshly ground black pepper

1. Add the chicken, broth, zucchini, celery, carrots, garlic, cumin, salt, and pepper to the slow cooker. Stir to mix well.

2. Cook on low for 4 to 6 hours or on high for 2 to 3 hours.

3. Remove the chicken from the slow cooker, shred it, toss it back into the soup, and serve.

Make it faster: Use the Pressure Cooker function on your Instant Pot. Add the ingredients to the Instant Pot and cook for 9 minutes on Manual. Use a natural release before opening the top and serving.

PER SERVING: Calories: 241; Fat: 8g; Carbohydrates: 13g; Fiber: 3g; Protein: 32g; Sodium: 549mg

Chicken Fajita Soup

Serves 4 / **Prep time:** 10 minutes / **Cook time:** 6 to 8 hours on low / 3 to 4 hours on high

Throw out that tortilla and pull out a spoon—your favorite fajita just went low-carb. When you make this from scratch instead of with processed foods, you'll discover that cooking with healthier ingredients tastes better than you ever imagined.

2 pounds boneless, skinless chicken thighs

2 bell peppers, seeded and sliced

1 onion, sliced

1 (28-ounce) can low-sodium or no-salt-added diced tomatoes

2 teaspoons chili powder

1 teaspoon ground cumin

½ teaspoon paprika

½ teaspoon salt

½ teaspoon freshly ground black pepper

⅛ teaspoon garlic powder

⅛ teaspoon onion powder

⅛ teaspoon oregano

⅛ teaspoon red pepper flakes

1. Add the chicken, bell peppers, onion, tomatoes, chili powder, cumin, paprika, salt, black pepper, garlic powder, onion powder, oregano, and red pepper flakes to a slow cooker. Stir to mix well.

2. Cook on low for 6 to 8 hours or on high for 3 to 4 hours.

Make it keto: Add classic fajita toppings to this soup, like shredded cheese and sour cream, for higher fat content.

Ingredient tip: The flavor punch of this recipe comes from what is essentially a homemade fajita seasoning mix. It's not only healthier (with no added ingredients) than the store-bought packet, but you probably already have all the spices in your pantry. Use this seasoning—ingredients chili powder through red pepper flakes—on more than just fajitas. Try tacos, enchiladas, and salads. Two-and-a-half tablespoons will season approximately 1½ to 2 pounds of meat. The mix will store in an airtight container for up to 3 months.

PER SERVING: Calories: 279; Fat: 7g; Carbohydrates: 18g; Fiber: 4g; Protein: 35g; Sodium: 579mg

Chicken Avocado Soup

Serves 6 / **Prep time:** 5 minutes / **Cook time:** 4 to 6 hours on low / 2 to 3 hours on high

This is a classic and comforting chicken soup with just a touch of Latin-inspired flair in the form of avocado, cilantro, and lime juice. It is so simple and yet incredibly delicious. Save the chicken bones in the freezer, and when you have enough, make your own Chicken Stock (page 122).

1 pound bone-in chicken breast

8 cups low-sodium chicken broth

2 scallions (whites and greens), sliced

1 tomato, diced

1 celery stalk, sliced

2 garlic cloves, minced

¼ teaspoon cumin

1 teaspoon salt

1 teaspoon freshly ground black pepper

1 tablespoon freshly squeezed lime juice

¼ cup chopped fresh cilantro , plus additional whole cilantro leaves for garnish

2 avocados, sliced

Lime wedges, for garnish

1. Add the chicken, broth, scallions, tomato, celery, garlic, cumin, salt, pepper, lime juice, and cilantro to a slow cooker.

2. Cook on low for 4 to 6 hours or on high for 2 to 3 hours.

3. Remove the chicken, shred the meat from the bones, and add the shredded meat back into the slow cooker. Stir to combine.

4. Ladle into 6 bowls and top with avocado slices.

5. Serve with lime wedges on the side.

Make it keto: Stir in ½ cup heavy (whipping) cream along with the shredded chicken.

PER SERVING: Calories: 257; Fat: 14g; Carbohydrates: 13g; Fiber: 6g; Protein: 25g; Sodium: 521mg

Turkey Slaw Soup

Serves 6 / **Prep time:** 5 minutes / **Cook time:** 6 to 8 hours on low / 3 to 4 hours on high

This is a spin on my popular "slawghetti" recipe. I took the main elements—meat and broccoli slaw—and turned it into a soup for an easy low-carb, Whole30, and paleo recipe.

1 pound 93% lean ground turkey

1 (12-ounce) package broccoli slaw

4 cups Chicken Stock (page 122)

1 (15-ounce) can low-sodium or no-salt-added diced tomatoes

1 small onion, diced

2 garlic cloves, minced

1 tablespoon Italian seasoning

1 teaspoon salt

½ teaspoon freshly ground black pepper

Handful chopped fresh parsley for garnish (optional)

1. Add the turkey, broccoli slaw, stock, tomatoes, onion, garlic, Italian seasoning, salt, and pepper to a slow cooker. Stir to mix well.

2. Cook on low for 6 to 8 hours or on high for 3 to 4 hours. Garnish with parsley, if using.

Make it keto: Stir in ½ cup half and half after it's done cooking. It will be deliciously creamy.

PER SERVING: Calories: 229; Fat: 8g; Carbohydrates: 17g; Fiber: 3g; Protein: 23g; Sodium: 790mg

Cheeseburger Soup

Serves 6 / **Prep time:** 10 minutes / **Cook time:** 6 to 8 hours on low / 3 to 4 hours on high

It's a cheeseburger in a bowl! Creamy and delightfully cheesy, this is the perfect comfort food. And you won't miss the bun as it fills you up with its bacony goodness.

1 pound 93% lean ground beef

4 cups low-sodium beef broth

1 small onion, diced

2 cloves garlic, minced

1 (15-ounce) can low-sodium or no-salt-added diced tomatoes

2 tablespoons Dijon mustard

2 tablespoons Worcestershire sauce

1 teaspoon dried parsley

½ teaspoon salt

¼ teaspoon freshly ground black pepper

1½ cups shredded Cheddar cheese

1 cup reduced-fat 2% milk

6 ounces bacon, cooked and crumbled

1. Add the beef, broth, onion, garlic, tomatoes, mustard, Worcestershire sauce, parsley, salt, and pepper to the slow cooker. Stir to mix well.

2. Cook on low for 6 to 8 hours or on high for 3 to 4 hours.

3. Stir in the cheese and the milk, and cook on high for 1 additional hour.

4. Top with the bacon before serving.

Ingredient tip: Dollop spoonfuls of your favorite burger toppings, like relish or Ketchup (page 130), into each soup bowl before serving.

Make it keto: Use heavy (whipping) cream instead of 2% milk.

PER SERVING: Calories: 436; Fat: 28g; Carbohydrates: 14g; Fiber: 2g; Protein: 32g; Sodium: 900mg

Zuppa Toscana with Cauliflower

Serves 6 / **Prep time:** 10 minutes / **Cook time:** 4 to 6 hours on low / 2 to 3 hours on high

Zuppa Toscana means literally "Tuscan soup," and although the ingredients change depending on what is available at the market, it usually includes sausage and potatoes. Here, cauliflower replaces the potatoes to lower the carbs. I've found this recipe adapts really well to cooking in a slow cooker, and it makes great leftovers, too.

1 pound Italian sausage

1 tablespoon extra-virgin olive oil

1 small onion, diced

3 garlic cloves, minced

4½ cups low-sodium chicken broth

1 large head cauliflower, cut into small florets

3 cups chopped kale

1 teaspoon salt

½ teaspoon freshly ground black pepper

¼ teaspoon red pepper flakes

½ cup heavy (whipping) cream

1. Add the sausage, olive oil, onion, garlic, broth, cauliflower, kale, salt, black pepper, and red pepper flakes to the slow cooker. Stir to mix well.

2. Cook on low for 4 to 6 hours or on high for 2 to 3 hours.

3. Stir in the cream and serve.

Ingredient tip: Brown the sausage ahead of time and drain the grease before adding to the slow cooker to cut the fat content. Mild or hot Italian sausages both work well with this recipe.

PER SERVING: Calories: 338; Fat: 25g; Carbohydrates: 12g; Fiber: 3g; Protein: 19g; Sodium: 877mg

Kofta Soup

Serves 4 / **Prep time:** 15 minutes / **Cook time:** 6 to 8 hours on low / 3 to 4 hours on high

Kofta is a Middle Eastern meatball. I love food from this region of the world because it always has so much flavor, and this meatball soup is a good example. Herbs and spices, like coriander, cumin, nutmeg, and mint, give it an incredible aroma, too.

1 pound 93% lean ground beef

1 small onion, diced

2 garlic cloves, minced

1 tablespoon parsley

2 teaspoons coriander

1 teaspoon cumin

½ teaspoon salt

½ teaspoon freshly ground black pepper

¼ teaspoon nutmeg

¼ teaspoon mint

¼ teaspoon paprika

5 cups low-sodium beef broth

1 cup cauliflower florets

2 carrots, diced

2 tablespoons tomato paste

1. In a large bowl, mix together the beef, onion, garlic, parsley, coriander, cumin, salt, pepper, nutmeg, mint, and paprika until well blended.

2. Using your hands, form meatballs about 1 inch in diameter, and place them on a large plate.

3. In a slow cooker, mix together the broth, cauliflower, carrots, and tomato paste.

4. Add the meatballs and cook on low for 6 to 8 hours or on high for 3 to 4 hours.

Make-ahead tip: Mix together the meatball ingredients and form into meatballs. Place the meatballs on a baking sheet, making sure they don't touch one another. Freeze for 1 hour, transfer to a large zip-top plastic bag, and freeze for up to 3 months. When ready to use them, add the soup ingredients and the frozen meatballs to the slow cooker, and cook on on low for 6 to 8 hours or high for 3 to 4 hours.

Substitution tip: Instead of the ground beef, try using ground chicken, turkey, or pork, which all go really well with the herbs and spices.

PER SERVING: Calories: 232; Fat: 8g; Carbohydrates: 10g; Fiber: 2g; Protein: 29g; Sodium: 579mg

Egg Roll Soup

Serves 4 / **Prep time:** 10 minutes / **Cook time:** 6 to 8 hours on low / 3 to 4 hours on high

Think of this as an egg roll without the wrapper. The wonderful flavors of the egg roll filling are all here: meat, cabbage, carrots, and a little soy sauce. No fancy ingredients to buy, and the best part is that it reheats well, so plan to bring leftovers to work for lunch.

1 pound 93% lean ground beef

5 cups low-sodium beef, chicken, or vegetable broth

1 small onion, diced

1 (12-ounce) package broccoli slaw

8 ounces green cabbage, shredded

1 teaspoon sesame oil (regular or toasted)

2 scallions (whites and greens), sliced

¼ cup low-sodium soy sauce or coconut aminos

¼ cup rice wine vinegar

½ teaspoon salt

¼ teaspoon freshly ground black pepper

3 garlic cloves, minced

1 tablespoon minced fresh ginger

1. Add the beef, broth, onion, slaw, cabbage, sesame oil, scallions, soy sauce, vinegar, salt, pepper, garlic, and ginger to a slow cooker.

2. Cook on low for 6 to 8 hours or on high for 3 to 4 hours.

Substitution tip: Use whatever ground meat you prefer: pork, beef, chicken, or turkey. Look for the leanest ground meat to minimize the amount of fat when it cooks.

PER SERVING: Calories: 297; Fat: 11g; Carbohydrates: 18g; Fiber: 4g; Protein: 34g; Sodium: 912mg

Cabbage Roll Soup

Serves 6 / **Prep time:** 5 minutes / **Cook time:** 6 to 8 hours on low / 3 to 4 hours on high

No need to fuss around with stuffing and rolling cabbage; here I've turned it into an easy-to-make soup that tastes of all the wonderful flavors normally found in a traditional cabbage roll. To keep the carbs down, I've replaced the rice that is usually in a cabbage roll with cauliflower that has been grated to resemble rice. This recipe works for those following the paleo or Whole30 diet, too.

2 cups chopped cabbage

1 pound 93% lean ground beef

2 cups riced cauliflower

1 (28-ounce) can low-sodium or no-salt-added diced tomatoes

½ cup low-sodium beef broth

1 small onion, diced

3 garlic cloves, minced

1 tablespoon Italian seasoning

½ teaspoon salt

½ teaspoon freshly ground black pepper

1. Add the cabbage, beef, cauliflower, tomatoes, broth, onion, garlic, Italian seasoning, salt, and pepper to a slow cooker. Stir to mix well.

2. Cook on low for 6 to 8 hours or on high for 3 to 4 hours.

Make it faster: Add the ingredients to an Instant Pot and cook on Manual for 10 minutes. Release the pressure naturally.

Substitution tip: Although this recipe is traditionally made with ground beef, it's also good with ground pork, chicken, or turkey.

PER SERVING: Calories: 245; Fat: 6g; Carbohydrates: 18g; Fiber: 5g; Protein: 26g; Sodium: 502mg

Beefy Pepper Soup

Serves 6 / **Prep time:** 5 minutes / **Cook time:** 6 to 8 hours on low / 3 to 4 hours on high

Bell peppers and ground beef are good flavor friends, and when you put them together with crushed tomatoes and cauliflower rice, you have a thick, hearty, low-carb meal that will keep you going all day. Bonus: The soup is naturally keto- and paleo-compliant.

1 bell pepper, seeded and chopped

1 pound 93% lean ground beef

1 onion, diced

1 tablespoon Italian seasoning

1 (28-ounce) can crushed tomatoes

2 cups low-sodium beef broth

¼ cup Ketchup (page 130)

2 cups riced cauliflower

½ teaspoon salt

¼ teaspoon freshly ground black pepper

1. Add the bell pepper, beef, onion, Italian seasoning, tomatoes, broth, ketchup, cauliflower, salt, and black pepper to a slow cooker. Stir to mix well.

2. Cook on low for 6 to 8 hours or on high for 3 to 4 hours.

Make-ahead tip: Buy frozen cauliflower rice and you'll save yourself some time doing all that grating.

Substitution tip: Use ground chicken or turkey in place of the ground beef. You can also use a 50/50 combination of ground beef and bulk sausage to really amp up the flavor.

PER SERVING: Calories: 187; Fat: 6g; Carbohydrates: 15g; Fiber: 4g; Protein: 20g; Sodium: 572mg

Beef and Mushroom Stew

Serves 6 / **Prep time:** 10 minutes / **Cook time:** 6 to 8 hours on low / 3 to 4 hours on high

Bacon and beef = a winning low-carb combo. This will fill up your kitchen with the intoxicating aroma of bacon, and you will not be able to resist its meaty charms. You can turn this stew into a soup by adding a few more cups of broth.

2 pounds beef stew meat

8 ounces bacon, cooked and crumbled

2 cups Bone Broth (page 121)

4 mushrooms, sliced

2 carrots, peeled and diced

1 onion, diced

1 teaspoon salt

1 teaspoon rosemary

¼ teaspoon freshly ground black pepper

1. Add the beef, bacon, broth, mushrooms, carrots, onion, salt, rosemary, and pepper to a slow cooker. Stir to mix well.

2. Cook on low for 6 to 8 hours or on high for 3 to 4 hours.

Ingredient tip: If you like really thick stew, add 1 teaspoon of xanthan gum after the initial cooking time and cook for an additional 10 to 15 minutes.

PER SERVING: Calories: 317; Fat: 12g; Carbohydrates: 6g; Fiber: 2g; Protein: 52g; Sodium: 547mg

Bean-Free Chili

Serves 4 / **Prep time:** 10 minutes / **Cook time:** 6 to 8 hours on low / 3 to 4 hours on high

Slow cookers were made for chili. The low-and-slow method meshes and then brings out the flavors of every ingredient. There are tons of chili recipes out there, and most of them have beans, which are high in carbs, so I've made this a meat-only chili. If you'd like to make this heartier, try adding more bell pepper and celery. This chili also happens to be paleo- and Whole30-compliant.

1½ pounds 93% lean ground beef

8 ounces tomato paste

1 (15-ounce) can low-sodium or no-salt-added diced tomatoes

1 small onion, chopped

1 bell pepper, seeded and chopped

2 celery stalks, chopped

1½ teaspoons cumin

1½ teaspoons chili powder

½ teaspoon freshly ground black pepper

½ teaspoon salt

1. Add the beef, tomato paste, diced tomatoes, onion, bell pepper, celery, cumin, chili powder, black pepper, and salt to the slow cooker. Stir to mix well.

2. Cook on low for 6 to 8 hours or on high for 3 to 4 hours.

Ingredient tip: Garnish this chili with your favorite low-carb toppings, like cheese and sour cream.

PER SERVING: Calories: 351; Fat: 12g; Carbohydrates: 18g; Fiber: 4g; Protein: 40g; Sodium: 636mg

Seafood
Low-Country
Boil, page 66

meatless & seafood

Kale Lasagna ✗

Serves 6 / **Prep time:** 15 minutes / **Cook time:** 4 to 6 hours on low / 2 to 3 hours on high

Instead of noodles, this vegetarian lasagna is layered with chopped kale, making it a lightened-up, low-carb-friendly version of this popular, classic comfort dish. Kale leaves are tough enough to stand up to the low-and-slow cooking method of the slow cooker.

Cooking spray

1 (28-ounce) can low-sodium or no-salt-added diced tomatoes

1 small onion, diced

2 teaspoons Italian seasoning

½ teaspoon salt

½ teaspoon freshly ground black pepper

1 pound kale, chopped

4 cups part-skim mozzarella cheese

Chopped fresh parsley, for garnish (optional)

1. Coat a slow cooker generously with cooking spray.

2. In a medium bowl, mix together the tomatoes, onion, Italian seasoning, salt, and pepper.

3. Place ¼ of the kale in the bottom of the slow cooker. Top with ¼ of the sauce mixture, followed by ¼ of the cheese. Repeat the layers until all the ingredients are used, ending with the cheese.

4. Cook on low for 4 to 6 hours or on high for 2 to 3 hours.

5. Garnish with parsley, if using.

Ingredient tip: Add your favorite diced vegetables to this lasagna, like mushrooms, bell peppers, or zucchini. The more, the merrier.

PER SERVING: Calories: 252; Fat: 12g; Carbohydrates: 19g; Fiber: 3g; Protein: 18g; Sodium: 801mg

Spaghetti Squash Pizza Casserole

Serves 6 / **Prep time:** 15 minutes / **Cook time:** 4 to 6 hours on low / 2 to 3 hours on high

Spaghetti squash is a popular low-carb alternative to spaghetti. This unique vegetable not only looks like spaghetti in appearance, but it has a mild taste, so you can use it in many different types of recipes—even this spin on pizza.

1 (2-pound) spaghetti squash

1 cup low-sodium or no-salt-added diced tomatoes

2 ounces olives, sliced

4 ounces mushrooms, sliced

1 bell pepper, seeded and diced

¼ cup diced onion

1½ tablespoons pizza seasoning

2 garlic cloves, minced

½ teaspoon salt

Cooking spray

2 cups shredded whole-milk mozzarella cheese

1. Pierce the spaghetti squash all over with a knife, place in a microwave-safe dish, and cook for 7 to 10 minutes, or until soft. Be careful removing the squash from the microwave because it will be very hot.

2. Cut the squash in half and scoop out and discard the seeds.

3. Use a fork to scrape out the spaghetti-like strands into a large bowl.

4. Add the tomatoes, olives, mushrooms, pepper, onion, pizza seasoning, garlic, and salt to the bowl, and mix together.

5. Coat a slow cooker generously with cooking spray.

6. Add the spaghetti squash mixture to the slow cooker. Top with the cheese.

7. Cook on low for 4 to 6 hours or on high for 2 to 3 hours.

Ingredient tip: Use whatever low-carb pizza toppings you prefer, like spinach or even artichoke.

PER SERVING: Calories: 328; Fat: 19g; Carbohydrates: 19g; Fiber: 5g; Protein: 23g; Sodium: 876mg

Indian Cauliflower Bake ⚓

Serves 6 / **Prep time:** 10 minutes / **Cook time:** 4 to 6 hours on low / 2 to 3 hours on high

Your kitchen will smell so good when you make this. Garam masala is an Indian spice mixture made up of ingredients that change from region to region. When this starts to cook, you might think there won't be enough sauce, but the tomatoes cook down and release their liquid. When the time comes, it will be just right.

Cooking spray

4 cups chopped cauliflower

1 (15-ounce) can low-sodium or no-salt-added diced tomatoes

1 cup coconut milk

1 small onion, diced

1 bell pepper, diced

2 carrots, diced

2 garlic cloves, minced

1 tablespoon garam masala

½ teaspoon salt

½ teaspoon ground ginger

½ teaspoon cumin

¼ teaspoon turmeric

¼ teaspoon cinnamon

2 tablespoons Ghee (page 129)

1 cup crumbled paneer (see Ingredient tip)

1. Coat a slow cooker generously with cooking spray.

2. Add the cauliflower, tomatoes, coconut milk, onion, bell pepper, carrots, garlic, garam masala, salt, ginger, cumin, turmeric, and cinnamon to the slow cooker. Stir to mix well.

3. Drizzle the ghee over the top.

4. Cook on low for 4 for 6 hours or on high for 2 to 3 hours. Sprinkle the cheese on top of the casserole for the last 10 to 15 minutes of cook time.

Substitution tip: Use curry powder instead of garam masala, if you like. Curry is a little milder, but it is harmonious with all the other ingredients in this recipe.

Ingredient tip: If you can't find paneer, try queso fresco, a semisoft fresh Mexican cheese similar in texture and flavor to paneer.

PER SERVING: Calories: 255; Fat: 18g; Carbohydrates: 17g; Fiber: 5g; Protein: 9g; Sodium: 488mg

Spinach Artichoke Casserole

Serves 6 / **Prep time:** 10 minutes / **Cook time:** 4 to 6 hours on low / 2 to 3 hours on high

Remember that spinach artichoke dip that everyone loves so much at holiday parties? This recipe takes those flavors, lowers the carbs by including cauliflower and zucchini, and turns it into a delicious main-course casserole.

Cooking spray

10 ounces fresh spinach, chopped

1 (15-ounce) can artichoke hearts, drained and chopped

2 cups chopped cauliflower

½ cup diced zucchini

2 cups shredded part-skim mozzarella cheese

8 ounces low-fat cream cheese, cut into small pieces if in brick form

1 cup whole-milk Greek yogurt

⅓ cup grated Parmesan cheese

2 garlic cloves, minced

½ teaspoon salt

½ teaspoon freshly ground black pepper

1. Coat a slow cooker generously with cooking spray.

2. Add the spinach, artichoke hearts, cauliflower, zucchini, mozzarella, cream cheese, yogurt, Parmesan, garlic, salt, and pepper to the slow cooker. Stir to mix well.

3. Cook on low for 4 to 6 hours or on high for 2 to 3 hours.

Substitution tip: Make this recipe without the cauliflower and zucchini and serve it as a dip at your next potluck. Cut the cauliflower into florets and cut the zucchini into sticks, and use them as the dippers.

PER SERVING: Calories: 294; Fat: 17g; Carbohydrates: 17g; Fiber: 4g; Protein: 20g; Sodium: 850mg

Stuffed Portobello Mushrooms

Serves 6 / **Prep time:** 10 minutes / **Cook time:** 4 to 6 hours on low / 2 to 3 hours on high

Portobello mushrooms are large and firm, which makes them good for stuffing and cooking in a slow cooker. I used a combination of zucchini, bell pepper, and onion for the stuffing, but you can get creative with this by adding other vegetables, like carrots or diced eggplant.

1 (28-ounce) can low-sodium or no-salt-added diced or crushed tomatoes

1 garlic clove, minced

1 teaspoon paprika

½ teaspoon salt

½ teaspoon freshly ground black pepper

½ teaspoon dried thyme

3 large portobello mushroom caps

1 tablespoon extra-virgin olive oil

1 medium zucchini, chopped

1 bell pepper, seeded and diced

1 small onion, diced

3 eggs

1⅓ cups shredded whole-milk mozzarella cheese

1. Add the tomatoes, garlic, paprika, salt, black pepper, and thyme to a slow cooker. Stir to mix well.

2. Rub the portobellos all over with the olive oil.

3. Mix together the zucchini, bell pepper, and onion in a medium bowl and divide the mixture evenly between the mushroom caps. Spoon a little of the tomato mixture on top of each mushroom.

4. Place the mushrooms in the slow cooker. Cook on low for 4 to 6 hours or on high for 2 to 3 hours.

5. Crack an egg over the top of each stuffed mushroom, sprinkle each with ⅓ cup of cheese, and cook on high for an additional 30 minutes, or until the egg is cooked to your liking.

Make it paleo or Whole30: Omit the mozzarella cheese.

PER SERVING: Calories: 241; Fat: 12g; Carbohydrates: 19g; Fiber: 4g; Protein: 15g; Sodium: 651mg

Thai Shrimp Soup

Serves 6 / **Prep time:** 10 minutes / **Cook time:** 4 to 6 hours on low / 2 to 3 hours on high

Coconut milk balances out the spiciness of the red curry paste, and together they give this seafood soup mouthwatering flavor that is more than the sum of its parts. It's also an extremely versatile recipe, so you can choose your favorite kind of fish or shellfish or whatever is freshest at the store. The soup is paleo- and Whole30-compliant, so it's great for everyone.

1 bell pepper, seeded and diced

1 small onion, diced

1 tablespoon red curry paste

Zest of 1 lemon

2 garlic cloves, minced

1 teaspoon salt

½ teaspoon ground ginger

½ teaspoon coriander

3¾ cups light coconut milk

2 cups Seafood Stock (page 123)

1½ pounds shelled fresh or frozen shrimp

2 tablespoons chopped fresh cilantro, for garnish

1. Add the bell pepper, onion, curry paste, lemon zest, garlic, salt, ginger, coriander, coconut milk, and stock to a slow cooker. Stir to mix well.

2. Cook on low for 4 to 6 hours or on high for 2 to 3 hours.

3. Add the shrimp and cook an additional 15 to 20 minutes on high, until the shrimp are cooked through.

4. Garnish with the cilantro.

Seafood tip: Substitute your favorite seafood (or seafood combination) for the shrimp, such as lobster, crab, or a firm white fish, like cod. Shells from cooked lobster and crab can be frozen and saved for Seafood Stock (page 123).

Ingredient tip: Red curry paste is usually found with the other Asian ingredients, like soy sauce, at grocery stores. But if you can't find it, add ¼ teaspoon red pepper flakes instead, which will give the recipe the mild spiciness that makes it taste so good.

PER SERVING: Calories: 390; Fat: 25g; Carbohydrates: 10g; Fiber: 2g; Protein: 24g; Sodium: 648mg

Seafood Low-Country Boil

Serves 8 / **Prep time:** 10 minutes / **Cook time:** 2 to 4 hours on low / 1 to 2 hours on high

A traditional low-country boil includes corn and potatoes, which are not a low-carb lover's friend, so I've left them out and amped up the flavor with kielbasa and lots of shrimp. Homemade Old Bay seasoning gives this dish the aromas and flavors of the South.

1 pound kielbasa sausage, cut into 1-inch pieces

5 cups water

1½ cups Vegetable Broth (page 120) or store-bought low-sodium vegetable broth

2 tablespoons Homemade Old Bay Seasoning (page 81)

2 lemons, sliced

2 celery stalks, chopped

1 onion, quartered

3 garlic cloves, minced

2 pounds fresh large shrimp in shells

1. Add the sausage, water, broth, seasoning, lemons, celery, onion, and garlic to the slow cooker.

2. Cook on low for 2 to 4 hours or on high for 1 to 2 hours.

3. Add the shrimp and cook an additional 15 to 20 minutes on high, or until the shrimp are cooked through.

Substitution tip: Instead of the 5 cups water, pour in 2½ cups coconut milk and 2½ cups water, which will add a different flavor and some good fat.

Ingredient tip: Large shrimp usually have 21 to 30 in a pound. Extra-large shrimp have 16 to 20 in a pound.

Seafood tip: A mixture of seafood also works well in this recipe. If you can find a prepackaged seafood medley at the grocery store, I suggest you try it.

PER SERVING: Calories: 299; Fat: 17g; Carbohydrates: 7g; Fiber: 2g; Protein: 30g; Sodium: 981mg

Shrimp Scampi Zoodles

Serves 4 / **Prep time:** 10 minutes / **Cook time:** 2 to 4 hours on low / 1 to 2 hours on high

Zucchini noodles cooked in the slow cooker are perfect for this super easy low-carb take on shrimp scampi. If you don't have a spiralizer to make zoodles, no problem: Use a vegetable peeler to cut the zucchini into lengthwise strips, then cut those into thin strands using a sharp knife.

4 cups low-sodium vegetable or chicken broth

2½ teaspoons lemon-garlic seasoning

1 small onion, chopped

1 tablespoon unsalted butter

2 medium zucchini, cut into spaghetti-like strands

1 pound shelled shrimp

1. Add the broth, lemon-garlic seasoning, onion, and butter to a slow cooker. Stir to mix well.

2. Add the zucchini to the slow cooker.

3. Cook on low for 2 to 4 hours or on high for 1 to 2 hours.

4. Add the shrimp and cook an additional 15 to 20 minutes on high, or until the shrimp are cooked through.

Seafood tip: Substitute your favorite shellfish. Crab or even crawfish can be used.

Make it paleo and Whole30: Replace the butter with Ghee (page 129).

PER SERVING: Calories: 217; Fat: 5g; Carbohydrates: 21g; Fiber: 5g; Protein: 25g; Sodium: 425mg

Cioppino

Serves 6 / **Prep time:** 10 minutes / **Cook time:** 6 to 8 hours on low / 3 to 4 hours on high

Packed with cod, scallops, mussels, and shrimp, this low-carb version of cioppino features the ease of the slow cooker, and it works for both paleo and Whole30 followers.

1 (28-ounce) can low-sodium or no-salt-added diced tomatoes

1 medium onion, diced

2 celery stalks, diced

1 bell pepper, seeded and diced

2 cups Seafood Stock (page 123)

4 garlic cloves, minced

2 teaspoons Italian seasoning

½ teaspoon red pepper flakes

1 bay leaf

1 tablespoon extra-virgin olive oil

1 pound cod fillets

8 ounces shrimp

8 ounces bay scallops

8 ounces mussels

Chopped fresh parsley (optional)

1. Add the tomatoes, onion, celery, bell pepper, stock, garlic, Italian seasoning, red pepper flakes, bay leaf, and olive oil to the slow cooker. Stir to mix well.

2. Cook on low for 6 to 8 hours or on high for 3 to 4 hours.

3. Add the cod, shrimp, scallops, and mussels. Cook on high for an additional 15 to 20 minutes.

4. Remove the bay leaf. Sprinkle the top with fresh parsley, if using.

Seafood tip: This recipe uses my favorite combination of seafood, but feel free to choose the fish and shellfish you like the best or what happens to be freshest at the grocery store. Just be sure to have a total of 2½ pounds, and you'll be good to go.

PER SERVING: Calories: 236; Fat: 4g; Carbohydrates: 19g; Fiber: 4g; Protein: 30g; Sodium: 745mg

Salmon with Lemon and Dill

Serves 4 / **Prep time:** 5 minutes / **Cook time:** 2 to 4 hours on low / 1 to 2 hours on high

Salmon cooks nicely in a slow cooker, leaving it moist and perfectly done. This is another dish with super low-carb status that's also good for paleo or Whole30 followers. What's not to like?

Cooking spray

2 pounds salmon fillets, skin removed

2 teaspoons extra-virgin olive oil

2 garlic cloves, minced

2 tablespoons chopped fresh dill

¼ teaspoon salt

¼ teaspoon freshly ground black pepper

1 lemon, sliced

1. Coat a slow cooker generously with cooking spray.

2. Rub the salmon with olive oil and sprinkle with the garlic, dill, salt, and pepper.

3. Place the salmon in the slow cooker. Top with the lemon slices.

4. Cook on low for 2 to 4 hours or on high for 1 to 2 hours.

Seafood tip: Good substitutes for salmon are Arctic char, mackerel, or bluefish.

PER SERVING: Calories: 327; Fat: 13g; Carbohydrates: 3g; Fiber: 1g; Protein: 51g; Sodium: 469mg

Thai Chicken Tacos, page 78

poultry

Bacon Ranch Chicken Casserole

Serves 6 / **Prep time:** 10 minutes / **Cook time:** 4 to 6 hours on low / 2 to 3 hours on high

This decadent recipe combines rich and satisfying ingredients, like bacon and cheese, into a comforting casserole the whole family will enjoy.

3 pounds boneless, skinless chicken thighs

4 ounces bacon, cooked and crumbled

8 ounces low-fat cream cheese

8 ounces low-fat sour cream

8 ounces Cheddar cheese, shredded

¼ cup diced onion

1 teaspoon garlic powder

1 teaspoon parsley

½ teaspoon salt

¼ teaspoon freshly ground black pepper

1. Add the chicken, bacon, cream cheese, sour cream, Cheddar, onion, garlic powder, parsley, salt, and pepper to a slow cooker. Stir to mix well.

2. Cook on low for 4 for 6 hours or on high for 2 to 3 hours.

Make it faster: Cook this in your Instant Pot: Add 1 cup Chicken Stock (page 122) along with the other ingredients and cook for 12 minutes. Use a manual release.

PER SERVING: Calories: 563; Fat: 32g; Carbohydrates: 8g; Fiber: 0g; Protein: 58g; Sodium: 831mg

Crack Chicken ✗

I call this Crack Chicken because once you taste it, you will be addicted—but in a good way! The shredded chicken is equally good served in lettuce wraps, on top of a salad, or as a main course with a simple side dish and a salad.

2 pounds boneless, skinless chicken breasts

½ cup water *broth?*

8 ounces low-fat cream cheese

2 tablespoons Homemade Ranch Seasoning (page 81)

6 slices bacon, cooked and chopped

1 cup shredded low-fat Cheddar cheese

1. Add the chicken, water, and cream cheese to a slow cooker. Sprinkle the ranch seasoning on top. Stir to mix well.

2. Cook on low for 4 to 6 hours or on high for 2 to 3 hours.

3. Remove the chicken and shred it using two forks.

4. Add the chicken back into the slow cooker along with the bacon. Stir to mix well. Top with the Cheddar cheese and serve.

Substitute tip: Use boneless, skinless thighs, which have a bit more fat and can stand up to longer cooking if you can't get back in time to turn off the slow cooker after the prescribed number of hours.

PER SERVING: Calories: 355; Fat: 19g; Carbohydrates: 4g; Fiber: 0g; Protein: 41g; Sodium: 752mg

Chicken Cordon Bleu ⚹

Serves 6 / **Prep time:** 10 minutes / **Cook time:** 4 to 6 hours on low / 2 to 3 hours on high

This is a deconstructed version of chicken cordon bleu made extra creamy by the mushroom sauce.

Cooking spray

2 pounds boneless, skinless chicken breasts

8 ounces uncured ham, sliced

8 ounces Swiss cheese, sliced

1¾ cups Cream of Mushroom Sauce (page 128)

1 tablespoon unsalted butter, cut into small pieces

1. Coat a slow cooker generously with cooking spray.

2. Place the chicken in the bottom of the slow cooker. Place the ham slices over the chicken. Place the cheese on top.

3. Pour the mushroom sauce over the top and spread it evenly with a spoon.

4. Scatter pieces of butter over the top.

5. Cook on low for 4 to 6 hours or on high for 2 to 3 hours.

Make-ahead tip: Make the mushroom sauce a day or two in advance and store it in the refrigerator, so it will be ready for this recipe.

PER SERVING: Calories: 345; Fat: 18g; Carbohydrates: 4g; Fiber: 1g; Protein: 40g; Sodium: 494mg

Caribbean Chicken Curry

Serves 6 / **Prep time:** 15 minutes / **Cook time:** 6 to 8 hours on low / 3 to 4 hours on high

This aromatic curry is packed with Caribbean flavors. Any dark-meat cut will do well here: legs, thighs, bone-in, boneless, skin-on, skinless. The nutritional information for the recipe was calculated using boneless, skinless chicken thighs.

3 pounds boneless, skin-on chicken thighs or other dark meat

1 onion, chopped

2 garlic cloves, minced

1 jalapeño pepper, chopped

½ cup coconut milk

1 tablespoon curry powder

1 teaspoon allspice

½ teaspoon cloves

½ teaspoon nutmeg

1 teaspoon ground ginger

1. Add the chicken, onion, garlic, jalapeño, coconut milk, curry powder, allspice, cloves, nutmeg, and ginger to a slow cooker. Stir to mix well.

2. Cook on low for 6 to 8 hours or on high for 3 to 4 hours.

Make-ahead tip: If you use chicken on the bone, after cooking, pull the meat from the bones and add the meat back to the slow cooker. Store the bones in a covered container in the refrigerator for up to 4 days or in the freezer for up to 6 months. When you've saved up enough bones, you can make Chicken Stock (page 122).

Make it keto: Swap in heavy (whipping) cream for the coconut milk and add a couple tablespoons of Ghee (page 129). Serve this over cauliflower rice.

PER SERVING: Calories: 328; Fat: 14g; Carbohydrates: 4g; Fiber: 1g; Protein: 45g; Sodium: 221mg

Chicken with Capers

Serves 4 / **Prep time:** 15 minutes / **Cook time:** 4 to 6 hours on low / 2 to 3 hours on high

Capers and lemon juice provide a light sauce for this chicken recipe that's also paleo and Whole30. Use your favorite cut of dark meat, whether it be legs, thighs, bone-in, boneless, skin-on, or skinless.

2 pounds boneless, skinless chicken legs or thighs

¼ cup freshly squeezed lemon juice

3 tablespoons capers, undrained

1 bay leaf

¾ cup Chicken Stock (page 122)

1. Add the chicken, lemon juice, capers, bay leaf, and stock to a slow cooker. Stir to mix well.

2. Cook on low for 4 to 6 hours or on high for 2 to 3 hours.

3. Remove bay leaf before serving.

Substitution tip: Make this creamier by substituting heavy (whipping) cream or half and half for the chicken broth.

PER SERVING: Calories: 295; Fat: 10g; Carbohydrates: 3g; Fiber: 1g; Protein: 56g; Sodium: 448mg

Za'atar Chicken

Serves 6 / **Prep time:** 5 minutes / **Cook time:** 4 to 6 hours on low / 2 to 3 hours on high

Za'atar is a Middle Eastern spice blend commonly consisting of dried thyme, oregano, and marjoram, which are mixed with toasted sesame seeds and salt. You can find it at Middle Eastern or Mediterranean specialty grocery stores or gourmet grocery stores, like Whole Foods, as well as online.

2 pounds bone-in, skin-on chicken thighs

2 tablespoons za'atar

⅓ cup water

Juice of 1 lemon

2 teaspoons extra-virgin olive oil

1 teaspoon white vinegar

1 teaspoon dried chopped onion

1 garlic clove, minced

½ teaspoon salt

¼ teaspoon freshly ground black pepper

1 lemon, sliced

1. Add the chicken to a slow cooker.

2. In a small bowl, mix together the za'atar, water, lemon juice, olive oil, vinegar, dried onion, garlic, salt, and pepper. Pour over the chicken in the slow cooker. Top with the lemon slices.

3. Cook on low for 4 to 6 hours or on high for 2 to 3 hours.

Ingredient tip: Add 1 pound zoodles (zucchini noodles) to this recipe during the last 30 minutes of cook time.

PER SERVING: Calories: 363; Fat: 27g; Carbohydrates: 3g; Fiber: 1g; Protein: 25g; Sodium: 384mg

Thai Chicken Tacos

Serves 6 / **Prep time:** 10 minutes / **Cook time:** 4 to 6 hours on low / 2 to 3 hours on high.

Everyone loves tacos. This unique version is inspired by Thai flavors and uses crunchy fresh lettuce leaves instead of carby taco shells.

2 pounds bone-in, skin-on chicken breasts

1 (15-ounce) can coconut milk

¼ cup chopped fresh cilantro

½ red onion, chopped, divided

3 garlic cloves, minced

1 tablespoon freshly squeezed lime juice

1 teaspoon minced fresh ginger

1 teaspoon turmeric

¾ teaspoon salt

½ teaspoon freshly ground black pepper

8 ounces butter lettuce leaves

Julienned carrots, for garnish

1 serrano pepper, sliced (optional)

1. Add the chicken, coconut milk, cilantro, half of the onion, garlic, lime juice, ginger, turmeric, salt, and black pepper to a slow cooker. Stir to mix well.

2. Cook on low for 4 to 6 hours or on high for 2 to 3 hours.

3. Remove the chicken from the slow cooker and shred the meat using two forks. Place the chicken back into the slow cooker and mix well.

4. Spoon the chicken mixture onto the lettuce leaves with the carrots, peppers (if using), and the remaining onion, wrap, and serve.

Ingredient tip: Serve these tacos topped with extra chopped cilantro and slices of avocado. Serrano peppers are quite hot, so if you don't like your food very spicy, leave it out or use a milder pepper, like a jalapeño or a poblano.

PER SERVING: Calories: 332; Fat: 19g; Carbohydrates: 5g; Fiber: 1g; Protein: 36g; Sodium: 369mg

Mississippi Chicken Thighs

Serves 6 / **Prep time:** 10 minutes / **Cook time:** 6 to 8 hours on low / 3 to 4 hours on high

This is my own variation of the famous Mississippi Roast recipe. Here, I've swapped out the beef for chicken thighs, and I call for homemade ranch mix and onion mix, which makes this much healthier. Ditching store-bought dressing packets and using my versions from scratch means you control what's in them, and you know that only natural ingredients are used.

3 pounds boneless, skinless chicken thighs

2 tablespoons Homemade Dry Onion Soup Mix (page 81)

2 tablespoons Homemade Ranch Seasoning (page 81)

8 whole pepperoncini peppers

4 tablespoons unsalted butter, cut into small pieces

1. Place the chicken thighs into the bottom of a slow cooker.
2. Sprinkle the dry onion mix and the ranch seasoning on top.
3. Add the pepperoncini, and scatter the butter pieces over the top.
4. Cook on low for 6 to 8 hours or on high for 3 to 4 hours.
5. Remove the chicken from the slow cooker and shred using two forks. Place the chicken back into the slow cooker and mix well.

Make it paleo, Whole30, and keto: Use Ghee (page 129) instead of butter.

PER SERVING: Calories: 354; Fat: 17g; Carbohydrates: 3g; Fiber: 0g; Protein: 45g; Sodium: 646mg

SEASONING MIXES MADE EASY

It's true that there's nothing easier than buying a packet of dry ranch or onion soup seasoning mix in your local grocery store, but making your own is nearly as easy, and it's far healthier. These are my go-to mixes. Old Bay seasoning is often used in Southern cooking, but when you make it yourself, it will be fresher and more flavorful. Ranch is a popular seasoning for a reason: It's not just flavorful, it's versatile, too. This homemade version can be used on meats and vegetables, or you can turn it into a dip. Most homemade ranch dressing comes in liquid form and uses buttermilk. Mine leaves out the liquid so you can store it in your pantry at room temperature. How handy is that? Homemade onion soup mix can be used to make not just sauces for slow cooker recipes but also salad dressings and even dips.

Homemade Old Bay Seasoning

Makes about 2 tablespoons /
Prep time: 5 minutes

2 teaspoons celery salt

1 teaspoon paprika

1 teaspoon mustard powder

½ teaspoon allspice

½ teaspoon freshly ground black pepper

½ teaspoon cardamom

¼ teaspoon cinnamon

¼ teaspoon ground ginger

¼ teaspoon cayenne pepper

Homemade Dry Onion Soup Mix

Makes about ½ cup / Prep time: 5 minutes

¼ cup dried chopped onion

1 tablespoon parsley

2 tablespoons onion powder

½ teaspoon freshly ground black pepper

1 teaspoon turmeric

1 teaspoon salt

1 teaspoon garlic powder

Homemade Ranch Seasoning

Makes about ½ cup / Prep time: 5 minutes

2 tablespoons dried chopped onion

1 teaspoon plus 1 teaspoon parsley

1 teaspoon plus 1 teaspoon chives

1 teaspoon plus 1 teaspoon dill

2½ teaspoons garlic powder

2½ teaspoons onion powder

2 teaspoons salt

For each mix, in a small bowl, combine the ingredients and stir well. Each mix will keep in a covered container at room temperature for up to 3 months.

Ingredient tip: To make the ranch seasoning into a dip, mix 2 tablespoons ranch seasoning mix with ½ cup low-fat sour cream. Let sit for at least 1 hour before serving so the flavors meld.

BBQ Chicken and Onions

Serves 10 / **Prep time:** 10 minutes / **Cook time:** 6 to 8 hours on low / 3 to 4 hours on high

This falling-off-the-bone chicken, flavored with homemade, low-carb barbecue sauce, is beyond delicious.

1 (3-pound) whole chicken

2 teaspoons extra-virgin olive oil

½ teaspoon salt

½ teaspoon freshly ground black pepper

1 large onion, sliced

2 cups BBQ Sauce (page 125)

1. Rub the chicken all over with the olive oil and season with the salt and pepper.

2. Place the onion slices into the bottom of a slow cooker. Place the chicken on top of the onion and pour the BBQ sauce all over the chicken.

3. Cook on low for 6 to 8 hours or on high for 3 to 4 hours.

Make-ahead tip: This chicken is perfect for repurposing in other recipes. Make the recipe ahead of time, store in a covered container in the refrigerator for up to 4 days, or freeze for up to 3 months.

Substitution tip: Make this recipe with cut chicken. This way you can choose all legs or all breasts—whatever part of the chicken you love the best. Lower the cook time by 1 hour if you use all-white meat, which cooks faster than dark meat.

PER SERVING: Calories: 370; Fat: 19g; Carbohydrates: 11g; Fiber: 4g; Protein: 39g; Sodium: 365mg

40-Garlic-Clove Chicken

Serves 4 / **Prep time:** 10 minutes / **Cook time:** 6 to 8 hours on low / 3 to 4 hours on high

Yes, there really are 40 cloves of garlic in this paleo- and Whole30-compliant recipe, but don't let that scare you. I know peeling all those cloves of garlic can be a large task—if you can find jarred, pre-peeled garlic cloves, use those instead. You really need to like garlic to enjoy this chicken recipe, but despite the amount of garlic I call for, it's not overpowering.

2 pounds bone-in, skin-on chicken legs or thighs (or a combination)

40 garlic cloves, peeled

1 cup Chicken Stock (page 122)

½ small onion, diced

1 teaspoon paprika

½ teaspoon salt

½ teaspoon freshly ground black pepper

1 bay leaf

1. Add the chicken, garlic, stock, onion, paprika, salt, pepper, and bay leaf to a slow cooker. Toss gently to coat the chicken.

2. Cook on low for 6 to 8 hours or on high for 3 to 4 hours. Discard the bay leaf before serving.

Make it keto: Swap out the stock for half and half or heavy (whipping) cream.

PER SERVING (USING CHICKEN LEGS): Calories: 346; Fat: 11g; Carbohydrates: 14g; Fiber: 2g; Protein: 47g; Sodium: 622mg

Tuscan Chicken

Serves 6 / **Prep time:** 10 minutes / **Cook time:** 6 to 8 hours on low / 3 to 4 hours on high

Here's a creamy chicken dish that's super easy, yet it's loaded with flavor. I like to serve this with mashed cauliflower and a simple salad for a complete meal.

2 pounds boneless, skinless chicken breasts or thighs

1½ cups whole milk

4 garlic cloves, minced

1 large shallot, minced

¼ cup white wine vinegar

2 tablespoons freshly squeezed lemon juice

1 tablespoon chopped fresh rosemary

1. Add the chicken, milk, garlic, shallot, vinegar, lemon juice, and rosemary to a slow cooker. Stir to mix well.

2. Cook on low for 6 to 8 hours or on high for 3 to 4 hours.

Make it keto: Use heavy (whipping) cream instead of milk.

Make it paleo and Whole30: Use Chicken Stock (page 122) in place of the milk.

PER SERVING (USING CHICKEN THIGHS): Calories: 271; Fat: 24g; Carbohydrates: 4g; Fiber: 0g; Protein: 12g; Sodium: 64mg

Chicken Saltimbocca

Serves 4 / **Prep time:** 10 minutes / **Cook time:** 4 to 6 hours on low / 2 to 3 hours on high

Saltimbocca is Italian for "jumps in the mouth" and refers to several dishes in which various meats are wrapped in ham. I've simplified it here and I think it's pretty darn good. Have a few toothpicks ready to secure the prosciutto around the chicken.

4 thin slices prosciutto (3 ounces total)

4 (6-ounce) boneless, skinless chicken breasts

1 cup Chicken Stock (page 122)

3 tablespoons capers

2 teaspoons dried rosemary

1. Wrap 1 slice of prosciutto around each chicken breast and secure with a toothpick. Place the wrapped chicken into the slow cooker.

2. Pour the stock over the chicken. Sprinkle with the capers and rosemary.

3. Cook on low for 4 to 6 hours or on high for 2 to 3 hours.

4. Discard toothpicks before serving.

Make it keto: Substitute 4 slices bacon for the prosciutto. Wrap 1 slice uncooked bacon around each chicken breast and secure it like you would with the prosciutto. Then cook as directed above.

PER SERVING: Calories: 271; Fat: 8g; Carbohydrates: 3g; Fiber: 1g; Protein: 45g; Sodium: 752mg

Mediterranean Stuffed Chicken Breasts

Serves 4 / **Prep time:** 15 minutes / **Cook time:** 4 to 6 hours on low / 2 to 3 hours on high

Mediterranean ingredients, like feta cheese and sun-dried tomatoes, are stuffed into chicken breasts and cooked low and slow until the flavors completely meld. Serve these for a dinner party or casual gathering along with a simple side dish of steamed carrots or broccoli. Have a few toothpicks at the ready to hold these together after they are stuffed.

4 ounces feta cheese, crumbled

⅓ cup chopped sun-dried tomatoes

4 garlic cloves, minced

2 teaspoons oregano

¼ teaspoon salt

⅛ teaspoon freshly ground black pepper

4 (6-ounce) boneless, skinless chicken breasts

2 tablespoons extra-virgin olive oil, divided

Cooking spray

1. In a small bowl, mix together the feta cheese, sun-dried tomatoes, garlic, oregano, salt, and pepper.

2. Place the chicken breasts between two pieces of plastic wrap and pound them with a meat mallet until they are about ¼ inch thick. Brush the chicken breasts with 1 tablespoon of olive oil. Sprinkle ¼ of the cheese mixture over each chicken breast. Roll up each piece starting from a short side; secure with toothpicks.

3. Coat a slow cooker generously with cooking spray. Place each stuffed chicken breast seam-side down in the slow cooker and brush with the remaining 1 tablespoon of olive oil.

4. Cook on low for 4 to 6 hours or on high for 2 to 3 hours.

5. Discard toothpicks before serving.

Make it paleo or Whole30: Omit the feta cheese.

PER SERVING: Calories: 335; Fat: 17g; Carbohydrates: 5g; Fiber: 1g; Protein: 45g; Sodium: 623mg

Turkey Joes

Serves 4 / **Prep time:** 10 minutes / **Cook time:** 4 to 6 hours on low / 2 to 3 hours on high

Watch this old-school classic go low-carb by cutting out some of the sloppy and serving it in lettuce leaves with a little cheese on top. It'll make you forget all about the cafeteria versions you're probably used to.

1½ pounds 93% lean ground turkey

6 ounces tomato paste

½ cup water

½ small onion, finely chopped

2 garlic cloves, minced

1 carrot, peeled and finely chopped

1 teaspoon paprika

1 teaspoon cayenne pepper

1 teaspoon cumin

½ teaspoon salt

¼ teaspoon freshly ground black pepper

8 lettuce leaves

1 cup shredded Cheddar cheese

1. Add the ground turkey, tomato paste, water, onion, garlic, carrot, paprika, cayenne, cumin, salt, and black pepper to a slow cooker. Stir to mix well.

2. Cook on low for 4 to 6 hours or on high for 2 to 3 hours.

3. To serve, spoon about ¼ cup of the turkey mixture on each lettuce leaf and top evenly with the cheese.

Ingredient tip: Use your favorite cheese instead of Cheddar or add some Ketchup (page 130).

PER SERVING: Calories: 408; Fat: 23g; Carbohydrates: 9g; Fiber: 2g; Protein: 42g; Sodium: 609mg

Turkey Spaghetti Squash Casserole

Serves 8 / **Prep time:** 10 minutes / **Cook time:** 6 to 8 hours on low / 3 to 4 hours on high

Spaghetti squash cooks directly in the slow cooker here with ground turkey, cheese, and herbs, resulting in a simple yet healthy main course. The spaghetti squash will be very hot. Be careful and use oven mitts.

2 pounds 93% lean ground turkey

1 (28-ounce) can low-sodium or no-salt-added diced tomatoes

¼ cup Parmesan cheese

1 cup shredded part-skim mozzarella cheese

1 small onion, diced

2 garlic cloves, minced

2 tablespoons Italian seasoning

½ teaspoon salt

1 (2-pound) spaghetti squash

Chopped fresh herbs, such as rosemary or thyme, for garnish (optional)

1. Add the turkey, tomatoes, Parmesan, mozzarella, onion, garlic, Italian seasoning, and salt to a slow cooker. Stir to mix well.

2. Halve the spaghetti squash crosswise and scoop out and discard the seeds. Place the halves cut-side down in the slow cooker.

3. Cook on low for 6 to 8 hours or on high for 3 to 4 hours.

4. Remove the spaghetti squash from the slow cooker, using oven mitts to protect your hands. Let the squash cool for about 5 minutes, then rake a fork across the flesh to remove it in spaghetti-like strands.

5. Add the spaghetti squash strands back into the slow cooker and mix until well combined. Garnish with fresh herbs, if using, and serve.

Ingredient tip: You'll know when the spaghetti squash is done when it is soft to the touch. You can also try ground beef or lamb.

Make it paleo and Whole30: Omit the cheese.

PER SERVING: Calories: 309; Fat: 12g; Carbohydrates: 20g; Fiber: 4g; Protein: 31g; Sodium: 515mg

Spicy Turkey Breast

Serves 8 / **Prep time:** 10 minutes / **Cook time:** 4 to 6 hours on low / 2 to 3 hours on high

Do you like your meals spicy? With jalapeños and a little cayenne, that's what you'll get in this low-carb, paleo, and Whole30 turkey dish. Cut it in slices and serve it as a weeknight meal for your family, or you can shred the meat and make lettuce-wrap tacos, or add it to a salad or soup. I also love this on top of mashed or riced cauliflower and some vegetables.

1 (3-pound) boneless, skinless turkey breast

2 jalapeños, sliced (see Ingredient tip)

½ cup water

1 teaspoon hot sauce

1 teaspoon cayenne pepper

1 teaspoon freshly ground black pepper

1 teaspoon garlic powder

1. Add the turkey and the jalapeños to a slow cooker.
2. In a small bowl, mix together the water, hot sauce, cayenne, black pepper, and garlic. Pour it over the top of the turkey.
3. Cook on low for 4 to 6 hours or on high for 2 to 3 hours.

Ingredient tip: If you truly like it spicy, use the whole jalapeño, seeds and all. If you like it a tad milder, cut out the seeds before adding to the slow cooker.

PER SERVING: Calories: 199; Fat: 3g; Carbohydrates: 1g; Fiber: 0g; Protein: 41g; Sodium: 206mg

BBQ Pork Ribs,
page 105

beef, pork & lamb

Beef Enchilada Casserole

Serves 6 / **Prep time:** 10 minutes / **Cook time:** 4 to 6 hours on low / 2 to 3 hours on high

Casseroles are known for being easy and convenient, but that doesn't mean they have to be boring. With cauliflower instead of rice and all the flavors of Mexico that you love, you'll make this satisfying meal all the time.

1 pound 93% lean ground beef

2 cups riced cauliflower

2 cups enchilada sauce

1 teaspoon chili powder

1 teaspoon paprika

½ teaspoon garlic powder

⅛ teaspoon freshly ground black pepper

4 ounces diced green chiles

4 ounces low-fat cream cheese

2 cups shredded Cheddar cheese

1. Add the beef, cauliflower, enchilada sauce, chili powder, paprika, garlic powder, black pepper, chiles, and cream cheese to a slow cooker. Stir to mix well.

2. Sprinkle the Cheddar cheese over the top.

3. Cook on low for 4 to 6 hours or on high for 2 to 3 hours.

Ingredient tip: You can also use ground turkey, chicken, or lamb. All taste really great in this casserole.

Make it paleo and Whole30: Omit the cream cheese and Cheddar cheese.

PER SERVING. Calories: 353; Fat: 21g; Carbohydrates: 13g; Fiber: 3g; Protein: 28g; Sodium: 1140mg

Mozzarella-Stuffed Meatballs

Serves 6 / **Prep time:** 15 minutes / **Cook time:** 4 to 6 hours on low / 2 to 3 hours on high

No bread crumbs here—almond flour and egg are used as the binding ingredients, so the carbs are lower and the dish is gluten-free. This is a good basic meatball recipe that can be used with other sauces. Or try serving over zoodles (zucchini noodles) or spaghetti squash.

1 pound 93% lean ground beef

1½ teaspoons Italian seasoning

1 large egg

2 tablespoons almond flour

½ teaspoon salt

¼ teaspoon freshly ground black pepper

8 ounces part-skim mozzarella, shredded

1 (28-ounce) can low-sodium or no-salt-added diced tomatoes

1. In a large bowl, mix together the beef, Italian seasoning, egg, almond flour, salt, and pepper. Using 2 to 4 tablespoons of the meatball mixture, form it into a ball and flatten it.

2. Place 1 to 3 teaspoons of the mozzarella on the center of the flattened meat. Form the meat around the mozzarella and shape into a ball. Repeat with the remaining meatball mixture and mozzarella.

3. Pour ½ of the tomatoes into a slow cooker. Add the meatballs. Cover the meatballs with the remaining tomatoes.

4. Cook on low for 4 to 6 hours or on high for 2 to 3 hours.

Make it paleo and Whole30: Omit the mozzarella.

PER SERVING: Calories: 326: Fat: 15g; Carbohydrates: 17g; Fiber: 3g; Protein: 30g; Sodium: 725mg

Beef and Mushroom Meatballs

Serves 6 / **Prep time:** 15 minutes / **Cook time:** 4 to 6 hours on low / 2 to 3 hours on high

Savory and filling, these meatballs make a great dinner on their own or on top of zoodles (zucchini noodles) or spaghetti squash. These are also paleo- and Whole30-compliant.

1 (28-ounce) can low-sodium or no-salt-added diced tomatoes

4 ounces mushrooms, finely chopped

1 small onion, finely chopped

2 garlic cloves, minced

1 tablespoon Italian seasoning

½ teaspoon salt

¼ teaspoon freshly ground black pepper

1 pound 93% lean ground beef

1. Pour the diced tomatoes in the bottom of a slow cooker.

2. In a medium bowl, combine the mushrooms, onion, garlic, Italian seasoning, salt, pepper, and beef. Mix until well blended.

3. Form into balls, using 2 to 4 tablespoons of the mixture for each meatball.

4. Add the meatballs to the slow cooker.

5. Cook on low for 4 to 6 hours or on high for 2 to 3 hours.

Make-ahead tip: Make the meatballs ahead of time and freeze them. Store these in a covered container or a large zip-top freezer bag in your freezer for up to 3 months. You can reheat them directly from the freezer, so dinner will be ready in a flash.

PER SERVING: Calories: 214; Fat: 6g; Carbohydrates: 14g; Fiber: 3g; Protein: 24g; Sodium: 461mg

Cuban Picadillo

Serves 4 / **Prep time:** 5 minutes / **Cook time:** 6 to 8 hours on low / 3 to 4 hours on high

Picadillo is a hash-like dish very popular in Latin American countries and in the Philippines. It's a nice dish to make for breakfast, lunch, or dinner. I like to serve it with a side of cauliflower rice.

1 pound 93% lean ground beef

½ cup low-sodium or no-salt-added diced tomatoes

½ cup pimento-stuffed green olives

½ tablespoon capers

½ small onion, diced

1 tablespoon tomato paste

½ teaspoon ground cumin

¼ teaspoon salt

⅛ teaspoon freshly ground black pepper

1. Add the ground beef, tomatoes, olives, capers, onion, tomato paste, cumin, salt, and pepper to a slow cooker. Stir to mix well.

2. Cook on low for 6 to 8 hours or on high for 3 to 4 hours.

Ingredient tip: Add a fried or poached egg to the top of each serving for an extra hearty meal. Or use the uncooked mixture in step 1 as a filling for bell peppers, place in a slow cooker, and cook for the same amount of time as above.

PER SERVING: Calories: 262; Fat: 14g; Carbohydrates: 4g; Fiber: 2g; Protein: 30g; Sodium: 698mg

Steak Bites †

Serves 6 / **Prep time:** 5 minutes / **Cook time:** 4 to 6 hours on low / 2 to 3 hours on high

This dish is completely wonderful on its own, but you can also jazz it up a bit by adding sliced onions, bell peppers, and mushrooms (or a combination of the three) along with the other ingredients. Since the meat is cut up into pieces, it does not need to cook as long as a larger piece of meat would.

2 pounds beef stew meat

½ cup Bone Broth (page 121)

¼ cup steak seasoning

2 tablespoons unsalted butter

1 tablespoon dried chopped onion

1 garlic clove, minced

¼ teaspoon salt (optional if your steak seasoning doesn't include it)

1. Add the beef, broth, steak seasoning, butter, dried onion, garlic, and salt (if using) to a slow cooker. Stir to mix well.

2. Cook on low for 4 to 6 hours or on high for 2 to 3 hours.

Make it faster: This is a good recipe for the Instant Pot. Sear the mushrooms and stew meat using the Sauté mode, add the remaining ingredients, and cook on Manual for 9 minutes. Use a manual release.

Make it paleo and Whole30: Substitute Ghee (page 129) for the butter.

PER SERVING: Calories: 331; Fat: 14g; Carbohydrates: 2g; Fiber: 0g; Protein: 51g; Sodium: 518mg

Bacon-Wrapped Meatloaf

Serves 8 / **Prep time:** 5 minutes / **Cook time:** 6 to 8 hours on low / 3 to 4 hours on high

Who doesn't love meatloaf? It's perfect for a family dinner, totally acceptable to order at a restaurant (be sure to ask if their recipe contains bread), and it's both paleo- and Whole30-compliant.

1 pound bacon

1 pound 93% lean ground beef

1 cup low-sodium or no-salt-added diced tomatoes

1 small egg

1 small onion, diced

2 garlic cloves, minced

¼ cup almond flour

1 tablespoon Italian seasoning

1 teaspoon salt

½ teaspoon freshly ground black pepper

1. Weave the bacon strips into a basket weave pattern and lie flat on a cutting board.

2. In a large bowl, mix together the ground beef, tomatoes, egg, onion, garlic, almond flour, Italian seasoning, salt, and pepper. Form the mixture into a rough loaf shape and place it on top of the woven bacon strips.

3. Wrap the bacon around the meatloaf, tucking the slices into the meat to secure. Place the bacon-wrapped meatloaf into a slow cooker, seam-side down.

4. Cook on low for 6 to 8 hours or on high for 3 to 4 hours.

5. If you want your bacon crisp, finish by placing the cooked bacon-wrapped meatloaf on a rimmed baking sheet and broil in the oven for 5 to 10 minutes.

Make it Whole30: Look for bacon that has no added sugar.

Make it keto: Sprinkle 1 cup shredded Cheddar cheese evenly across the top of the meatloaf before you wrap it in the bacon.

Ingredient tip: If you have leftovers, eat them for lunch the next day along with a simple side salad.

PER SERVING: Calories: 388; Fat: 29g; Carbohydrates: 6g; Fiber: 1g; Protein: 24g; Sodium: 760mg

Balsamic Beef Roast

Serves 6 / **Prep time:** 5 minutes / **Cook time:** 8 to 10 hours on low / 4 to 5 hours on high

Roasts love the low-and-slow method of cooking in a slow cooker. With very few ingredients, you can have a completely delicious beef roast packed with flavor. Make this when you need to impress some guests or you want a special family dinner. And by using the slow cooker, you can serve this even on busy weeknights.

½ cup low-sodium beef broth

⅓ cup balsamic vinegar

1 tablespoon Dijon mustard

1 (3-pound) boneless lean chuck roast, trimmed of fat

¼ teaspoon salt

¼ teaspoon freshly ground black pepper

4 carrots, peeled and chopped

1 medium onion, chopped

1. In a small bowl, whisk together the broth, balsamic vinegar, and mustard until well blended.

2. Season the roast with the salt and pepper and place in the bottom of a slow cooker. Place the carrots and onion around the roast.

3. Pour the broth mixture over the top.

4. Cook on low for 8 to 10 hours or on high for 4 to 5 hours.

Ingredient tip: This roast will be very tender when it's done cooking. Shred any leftover meat and use it in other dishes, like lettuce wraps, soups, or salads.

PER SERVING: Calories: 369; Fat: 15g; Carbohydrates: 9g; Fiber: 2g; Protein: 49g; Sodium: 387mg

Beef Shawarma Roast

Serves 8 / **Prep time:** 10 minutes / **Cook time:** 8 to 10 hours on low / 4 to 5 hours on high

Shawarma is usually made with chicken marinated in lemon juice, olive oil, and lots of spices. I've opted to use beef here, which can stand up to the long cooking time in the slow cooker. The result is a melt-in-your-mouth roast that will have your entire kitchen smelling amazing as it cooks. Rump, chuck, brisket ... use your cut of choice. Not only is this low-carb but it's paleo- and Whole30-friendly, as well.

1 small onion, sliced

3 garlic cloves, minced

1 (3-pound) boneless lean beef shoulder pot roast, trimmed of fat

¼ cup Bone Broth (page 121)

3 tablespoons white vinegar

3 tablespoons freshly squeezed lemon juice

2 tablespoons extra-virgin olive oil

1 tablespoon water

2 teaspoons allspice

1 teaspoon nutmeg

1 teaspoon cardamom

1 teaspoon garlic powder

½ teaspoon salt

½ teaspoon freshly ground black pepper

¼ teaspoon cinnamon

¼ cup finely chopped fresh parsley

1. Place the onion and garlic in the bottom of a slow cooker. Place the roast on top.

2. In a small bowl, mix together the broth, vinegar, lemon juice, olive oil, water, allspice, nutmeg, cardamom, garlic powder, salt, pepper, and cinnamon. Pour the sauce over the roast in the slow cooker.

3. Cook on low for 8 to 10 hours or on high for 4 to 5 hours.

4. Garnish with the parsley.

Make it faster: Use your Instant Pot. Follow the instructions above, use an additional ¾ cup bone broth, and cook on Manual for 30 minutes. Use a natural release.

Ingredient tip: The roast can be sliced and served or shredded using two forks.

PER SERVING: Calories: 250; Fat: 10g; Carbohydrates: 3g; Fiber: 1g; Protein: 38g; Sodium: 273mg

Philly Cheesesteak Wraps

Serves 6 / **Prep time:** 10 minutes / **Cook time:** 4 to 6 hours on low / 2 to 3 hours on high

I'll bet you didn't think you could eat a Philly cheesesteak on a low-carb diet. Lucky you, this recipe makes it possible—and it is so easy to make, you won't believe it. Everything, including the cheese, cooks together in the slow cooker.

2 pounds lean beef sirloin, sliced

2 bell peppers, seeded and sliced

1 large onion, sliced

4 ounces mushrooms, sliced

1 tablespoon Ghee (page 129)

⅓ cup low-sodium beef broth

1 teaspoon steak seasoning

½ teaspoon garlic powder

¼ teaspoon freshly ground black pepper

¼ teaspoon parsley

¼ teaspoon salt (optional if your steak seasoning doesn't include it)

6 slices provolone cheese

1 head iceberg lettuce

1. Add the beef, bell peppers, onion, mushrooms, ghee, broth, steak seasoning, garlic powder, black pepper, parsley, and salt (if using) to a slow cooker. Stir to mix well.

2. Cook on low for 4 to 6 hours or on high for 2 to 3 hours.

3. Stir to mix again and layer the provolone slices across the top of the mixture.

4. Cook an additional 10 to 15 minutes on high or until the cheese is melted. Spoon onto lettuce leaves, wrap, and serve immediately.

Make it paleo and Whole30: Omit the cheese.

PER SERVING: Calories: 318; Fat: 13g; Carbohydrates: 7g; Fiber: 2g; Protein: 42g; Sodium: 303mg

Chimichurri Pork and Bell Peppers

Serves 8 / **Prep time:** 5 minutes / **Cook time:** 8 to 10 hours on low / 4 to 5 hours on high

Chimichurri is an easy-to-make sauce of cilantro, parsley, and olive oil. Most people use it as a topping, probably because of its gorgeous green color, but you can also use it as a cooking sauce, like in this recipe. Since it is so flavorful, not many other ingredients are needed for flavor.

2½ pounds lean pork loin

2 bell peppers, seeded and chopped

1 small onion, chopped

½ teaspoon salt

¼ teaspoon freshly ground black pepper

1 cup Chimichurri Sauce (page 127)

1. Add the pork, bell peppers, onion, salt, and black pepper to a slow cooker. Pour the chimichurri over the top.
2. Cook on low for 8 to 10 hours or on high for 4 to 5 hours.

Substitution tip: I love pork loin, but lots of other cuts will work in this recipe, like chops or country-style ribs.

Make-ahead tip: Make the chimichurri and store it in the refrigerator or freezer, and it will be ready to use here.

PER SERVING: Calories: 343; Fat: 22g; Carbohydrates: 4g; Fiber: 1g; Protein: 31g; Sodium: 299mg

Jerk Pork Chops

Serves 4 / **Prep time:** 5 minutes / **Cook time:** 4 to 6 hours on low / 2 to 3 hours on high

Here I make use of homemade jerk seasoning to make this creamy pork chop recipe aromatic and flavorful without a lot of fuss. Overcooked pork chops will be dry, so pay attention to the cook times here, which will be similar to those of chicken breasts.

4 (6-ounce) bone-in pork chops, trimmed of fat

1 small onion, sliced

2 garlic cloves, minced

⅓ cup low-sodium chicken broth

1 teaspoon extra-virgin olive oil

1 teaspoon parsley

1 teaspoon dried chopped onion

½ teaspoon garlic powder

½ teaspoon thyme

½ teaspoon salt

½ teaspoon nutmeg

½ teaspoon allspice

½ teaspoon freshly ground black pepper

¼ teaspoon red pepper flakes

¼ teaspoon cayenne pepper

¼ teaspoon cinnamon

1. Place the pork chops, onion, and garlic into a slow cooker.

2. In a small bowl, mix together the broth, olive oil, parsley, dried onion, garlic powder, thyme, salt, nutmeg, allspice, black pepper, red pepper flakes, cayenne, and cinnamon. Pour the mixture over the pork chops.

3. Cook on low for 4 to 6 hours or on high for 2 to 3 hours.

Substitution tip: Instead of pork chops, use 1½ pounds chicken thighs and add 1 hour to the cook time on either low or high.

PER SERVING: Calories: 236; Fat: 6g; Carbohydrates: 4g; Fiber: 1g; Protein: 40g; Sodium: 348mg

Pork Marengo

Serves 6 / **Prep time:** 5 minutes / **Cook time:** 6 to 8 hours on low / 3 to 4 hours on high

Pork Marengo is a fancy name for pork and mushrooms cooked in gravy. The slow cooker version here produces succulent meat that's so tender, it falls apart. Both paleo- and Whole30-friendly, this dish makes an even more filling meal when served over mashed cauliflower or cauliflower rice.

2 pounds boneless lean pork shoulder, cut into 1-inch cubes

1 (15-ounce) can low-sodium or no-salt-added diced tomatoes

½ cup chopped onion

3 ounces mushrooms, finely chopped

1 garlic clove, minced

1 teaspoon marjoram

½ teaspoon thyme

1. Add the pork, tomatoes, onion, mushrooms, garlic, marjoram, and thyme to a slow cooker. Stir to mix well.

2. Cook on low 6 for 8 hours or on high for 3 to 4 hours.

Ingredient tip: If you want a thicker, stew-like consistency, mix together 3 tablespoons cornstarch and ⅓ cup water. Pour the mixture into the slow cooker at the end of the cook time and cook on high for an additional 5 to 10 minutes.

PER SERVING: Calories: 414; Fat: 27g; Carbohydrates: 8g; Fiber: 2g; Protein: 29g; Sodium: 213mg

Pork Carnitas

Serves 6 / **Prep time:** 10 minutes / **Cook time:** 6 to 8 hours on low / 3 to 4 hours on high

Carnitas is braised or roasted pork that is then shredded and used in lots of different dishes, like tacos and burritos. In addition to using the slow cooker here, the meat is also broiled briefly after cooking to make it a little crispy. Not only is this low-carb, but it's compliant to other similar diets, which makes it a go-to recipe for nearly everyone.

2 pounds boneless lean pork loin

1 teaspoon salt

½ teaspoon freshly ground black pepper

¾ cup low-sodium chicken broth

3 sprigs thyme

2 bay leaves

1 large sprig rosemary

1. Season the pork with the salt and pepper and place it in a slow cooker.

2. Add the broth, thyme, bay leaves, and rosemary, to the slow cooker.

3. Cook on low for 6 to 8 hours or on high for 3 to 4 hours.

4. Remove and discard the thyme and rosemary sprigs and the bay leaves. Transfer the meat to a cutting board and shred using two forks.

5. Spread out the shredded meat on a baking sheet and broil in the oven for 3 to 5 minutes, until crisp (but not burnt).

Ingredient tip: What to do with this meat? The sky is the limit: Lettuce wraps, cauliflower rice burrito bowls, or even over some mixed greens for a nice, low-carb salad. If you don't want crispy pork, omit the broiling step.

PER SERVING: Calories: 258; Fat: 13g; Carbohydrates: 1g; Fiber: 0 g; Protein: 33g; Sodium: 468mg

BBQ Pork Ribs

Serves 6 / **Prep time:** 10 minutes / **Cook time:** 7 to 8 hours on low / 3½ to 4 hours on high

Want ribs so tender they fall off the bone? Put them in the slow cooker. Using my homemade BBQ Sauce, this entire recipe is also paleo- and Whole30-compliant. This is a fantastic dish to bring to a summer picnic or a family reunion.

2½ pounds baby back ribs

1½ teaspoons garlic powder

1 teaspoon salt

1 teaspoon freshly ground black pepper

½ teaspoon paprika

1 onion, chopped

1 cup BBQ Sauce (page 125) divided

1. Season the ribs with the garlic powder, salt, pepper, and paprika. Place the ribs in a slow cooker, curved around the sides and standing up.
2. Add the onion to the center of the slow cooker.
3. Cook for 3 to 4 hours on low or 1½ to 2 hours on high.
4. Brush the ribs with ¾ cup of the sauce.
5. Cook for an additional 4 hours low or an additional 2 hours on high.
6. Place the ribs on a baking sheet and brush them with the remaining ¼ cup of sauce. Broil for 5 to 10 minutes, or until the outsides are crispy.

Ingredient tip: If you don't want crispy ribs, omit the broiling step.

PER SERVING: Calories: 370; Fat: 19g; Carbohydrates: 11g; Fiber: 4g; Protein: 42g; Sodium: 702mg

Lamb Kebab Casserole

Serves 6 / **Prep time:** 10 minutes / **Cook time:** 6 to 8 hours on low / 3 to 4 hours on high

Middle Eastern ingredients, like lamb, coriander, and mint, give this casserole kebab-like flavors that are filling yet still feel light. When you throw all the ingredients in the slow cooker, it won't look much like a casserole at first, but as it cooks, the ingredients meld into a saucy mix of mouthwatering goodness.

1 pound 85% lean ground lamb

2 cups riced cauliflower

1 (15-ounce) can low-sodium or no-salt-added diced tomatoes

1 small onion, diced

2 garlic cloves, minced

1 tablespoon parsley

2 teaspoons coriander

1 teaspoon cumin

½ teaspoon salt

½ teaspoon freshly ground black pepper

¼ teaspoon nutmeg

¼ teaspoon mint

¼ teaspoon paprika

8 ounces feta, crumbled

1. Add the ground lamb, cauliflower, tomatoes, onion, garlic, parsley, coriander, cumin, salt, pepper, nutmeg, mint, and paprika to a slow cooker. Stir to mix well.

2. Cook on low for 6 to 8 hours or on high for 3 to 4 hours.

3. Sprinkle the feta cheese over the top just before serving.

Make it paleo and Whole30: Omit the feta cheese.

Ingredient tip: Make this a well-rounded meal by serving it with a simple side salad of greens drizzled with oil and balsamic vinegar. Grocery stores carry frozen cauliflower rice, which you can use instead of grating a cauliflower yourself.

PER SERVING: Calories: 378; Fat: 27g; Carbohydrates: 12g; Fiber: 2g; Protein: 23g; Sodium: 834mg

Easy Lamb Tagine

Serves 6 / Prep time: 10 minutes / **Cook time:** 8 to 10 hours on low / 4 to 5 hours on high

A tagine is a common North African stew that uses a low-and-slow cooking method to produce melt-in-your-mouth meat with intense flavors and spices that's easily replicated by the slow cooker. While a tagine is traditionally served with pita, instead serve this over cauliflower rice with vegetables for a meal that will appeal to both paleo and Whole30 followers.

2 pounds lamb shanks

½ cup Bone Broth (page 121)

¼ cup raisins

1 onion, diced

4 garlic cloves, minced

2 tablespoons unsalted butter

2 teaspoons ground ginger

1½ teaspoons cumin

1 teaspoon paprika

½ teaspoon cayenne pepper

½ teaspoon salt

¼ teaspoon freshly ground black pepper

Cilantro sprigs, for garnish

1. Add the lamb, broth, raisins, onion, garlic, butter, ginger, cumin, paprika, and cayenne pepper, salt, and pepper to a slow cooker. Stir to mix well.

2. Cook on low for 8 to 10 hours or on high for 4 to 5 hours.

3. Garnish with cilantro sprigs.

Make it faster: Add all the ingredients except the cilantro sprigs, plus an additional ½ cup bone broth, to an Instant Pot and cook on Manual for 30 minutes. Use a natural release.

Substitution tip: Try other dried fruits, like dried blueberries.

PER SERVING: Calories: 257; Fat: 11g; Carbohydrates: 9g; Fiber: 1g; Protein: 32g; Sodium: 103mg

Blueberry Muffin Cake, page 110

desserts & sweet treats

Blueberry Muffin Cake

Serves 10 / **Prep time:** 15 minutes / **Cook time:** 4 to 6 hours on low / 2 to 3 hours on high

Is this a cake or a muffin? It's both. Serve this sweet, keto-friendly blueberry treat as an after-dinner dessert or as part of your next brunch spread.

Cooking spray

3 cups almond flour

½ cup 2% fat plain Greek yogurt

¼ cup powdered erythritol sweetener of your choice

3 large eggs

2 to 3 teaspoons grated lemon zest

1½ teaspoons baking powder

1 teaspoon vanilla extract

½ teaspoon baking soda

¼ teaspoon salt

1 cup fresh or frozen blueberries

1. Coat a slow cooker generously with cooking spray.

2. In a large bowl, mix together the almond flour, yogurt, erythritol, eggs, lemon zest, baking powder, vanilla, baking soda, and salt until well blended. Carefully fold in the blueberries.

3. Pour the batter into the slow cooker.

4. Place a paper towel between the slow cooker and the lid to cut down on any condensation that develops. Cook on low for 4 to 6 hours or on high for 2 to 3 hours, or until a toothpick inserted in the center comes out clean.

Substitution tip: Instead of blueberries, try raspberries or blackberries in the same amount. Or you can even use dried berries.

PER SERVING: Calories: 240; Fat: 19g; Carbohydrates: 13g; Fiber: 6g; Protein: 10g; Sodium: 202mg

Pecan Cookie

Serves 8 / **Prep time:** 10 minutes / **Cook time:** 4 to 6 hours on low / 2 to 3 hours on high

This will remind you of a buttery pecan sandie, but you can enjoy it guilt-free. It's another great option if you're following a keto diet, too.

Cooking spray

1¼ cup almond flour

⅔ cup powdered erythritol sweetener of your choice

⅓ cup chopped pecans

1 large egg

5 tablespoons unsalted butter, at room temperature

1 tablespoon coconut flour

1 teaspoon baking powder

½ teaspoon vanilla extract

1. Coat a slow cooker generously with cooking spray.

2. In a large bowl, mix together the almond flour, erythritol, pecans, egg, butter, coconut flour, baking powder, and vanilla until well blended. Pour the batter into the slow cooker.

3. Place a paper towel between the slow cooker and the lid to cut down on any condensation that develops. Cook on low for 4 to 6 hours or on high for 2 to 3 hours, or until a toothpick inserted in the center comes out clean.

Ingredient tip: Stir ¼ cup sugar-free chocolate chips into the batter to "sweeten" this up even more.

PER SERVING: Calories: 233; Fat: 20g; Carbohydrates: 16g; Fiber: 9g; Protein: 5g; Sodium: 60mg

Crustless Pumpkin Pie

Serves 4 / **Prep time:** 10 minutes / **Cook time:** 2 to 4 hours on low / 1 to 2 hours on high

The best part of pumpkin pie is the creamy filling loaded with aromatic spices. You'll never miss the crust, and you'll find yourself making this all year round, not just in the fall. Read the labels—look for 100% pure pumpkin, not pumpkin pie filling (which has other ingredients mixed in).

Cooking spray

1 (15-ounce) can pumpkin purée (without salt)

4 large eggs, beaten

½ cup whole milk

¼ cup powdered erythritol sweetener of your choice

1½ teaspoons vanilla

1 teaspoon pumpkin pie spice

½ teaspoon salt

1. Coat a slow cooker generously with cooking spray.

2. In a large bowl, mix together the pumpkin, eggs, milk, vanilla, erythritol, pumpkin pie spice, and salt. Spread the mixture evenly in the bottom of the slow cooker.

3. Place a paper towel between the slow cooker and the lid to cut down on any condensation that develops. Cook on low for 2 to 4 hours or on high for 1 to 2 hours.

Ingredient tip: This is terrific topped with fat-free or low-fat whipped topping.

Substitution tip: If you can't find pumpkin pie spice, mix together ½ teaspoon ground cinnamon, ¼ teaspoon ground ginger, ¼ teaspoon ground cloves, and ¼ teaspoon ground nutmeg.

PER SERVING: Calories: 150; Fat: 6g; Carbohydrates: 18g; Fiber: 8g; Protein: 8g; Sodium: 384mg

Strawberry Ricotta Cheesecake

Serves 4 / **Prep time:** 10 minutes / **Cook time:** 2 to 4 hours on low / 1 to 2 hours on high

A cheesecake cooked in a slow cooker is certainly not traditional, and neither is the missing crust, but you will absolutely love this low-carb version. This version uses my indulgent Strawberry Sauce and retains the creaminess of the original by using ricotta instead of cream cheese. Since this is cooked in the slow cooker, the end result will have a different texture than a regular cheesecake. The center should be firm rather than "almost set" like a traditional cheesecake.

Cooking spray

2 cups part-skim ricotta cheese

½ cup Strawberry Sauce (page 131)

2 large eggs

1 tablespoon plus 2 teaspoons powdered erythritol sweetener of your choice

1 teaspoon vanilla extract

1. Coat a slow cooker generously with cooking spray.

2. In a large bowl, mix together the ricotta, strawberry sauce, eggs, erythritol, and vanilla until well blended. Pour the mixture into the slow cooker.

3. Place a paper towel between the slow cooker and the lid to cut down on any condensation that develops. Cook on low for 2 to 4 hours or on high for 1 to 2 hours, or until a toothpick inserted into the center comes out clean.

Ingredient tip: Substitute 4 ounces sliced fresh strawberries for the Strawberry Sauce. Or garnish each slice with sliced strawberries.

PER SERVING: Calories: 223; Fat: 12g; Carbohydrates: 10g; Fiber: 1g; Protein: 18g; Sodium: 159m

Custard

Serves 4 / **Prep time:** 10 minutes / **Cook time:** 2 to 4 hours on low / 1 to 2 hours on high

This custard might look simple, but that's because it is. A silky, smooth custard is an impressive dessert, and that's what you'll find here.

Cooking spray

3 large eggs

2 cups half and half

¾ cup powdered erythritol sweetener of your choice

½ teaspoon vanilla extract

⅛ teaspoon nutmeg

1. Coat a slow cooker generously with cooking spray.

2. In a large bowl, mix together the eggs, half and half, erythritol, vanilla, and nutmeg. Spread the mixture evenly in the bottom of the slow cooker.

3. Place a paper towel between the slow cooker and the lid to cut down on any condensation that develops. Cook on low for 2 to 4 hours or on high for 1 to 2 hours, or until a toothpick inserted into the center comes out clean. Let cool before serving.

Ingredient tip: Top this dessert with your favorite berries. Strawberries, raspberries, and blackberries are good low-calorie options. Store leftover custard in a covered container in the refrigerator for up to 4 days.

PER SERVING: Calories: 235; Fat: 16g; Carbohydrates: 14g; Fiber: 0g; Protein: 9g; Sodium: 127mg

Brownies

Serves 9 / **Prep time:** 10 minutes / **Cook time:** 4 to 6 hours on low / 2 to 3 hours on high

Here is the brownie recipe you've been waiting for. This chocolaty treat will satisfy your sweet tooth without breaking your diet.

Cooking spray

¾ cup almond flour

¼ cup plus 2 tablespoons powdered erythritol sweetener of your choice

¼ cup unsweetened cocoa powder

½ teaspoon baking powder

4 large eggs

4 ounces low-fat cream cheese, softened

6 tablespoons unsalted butter, melted

1½ teaspoons vanilla extract

½ cup chocolate chips

1. Coat a slow cooker generously with cooking spray.

2. In a small bowl, mix together the almond flour, erythritol, cocoa powder, and baking powder and set aside.

3. In a large bowl, mix together the eggs, cream cheese, butter, and vanilla. Slowly stir in the almond flour mixture and mix to combine. Stir in the chocolate chips.

4. Pour the batter into the slow cooker.

5. Place a paper towel between the slow cooker and the lid to cut down on any condensation that develops. Cook on low for 4 to 6 hours or on high for 2 to 3 hours, or until a toothpick inserted in the center comes out clean.

Ingredient tip: Add chopped nuts to your brownies! Stir chopped walnuts, pecans, or almonds into the batter at the beginning of cook time.

PER SERVING: Calories: 261; Fat: 20g; Carbohydrates: 18g; Fiber: 6g; Protein: 7g; Sodium: 101mg

Strawberry Cobbler

Serves 8 / **Prep time:** 15 minutes / **Cook time:** 4 to 6 hours on low / 2 to 3 hours on high

Cobblers always remind me of my mother's kitchen. This healthy, low-carb cobbler is a lot easier than my mom's version but with the same delicious flavor. The end result is bubbling strawberry cobbler that will have your kitchen smelling amazing.

Cooking spray

2 cups fresh strawberries

3 tablespoons powdered erythritol sweetener of your choice, divided

1 large egg

½ cup coconut oil

1 teaspoon vanilla

1 cup coconut flour

1 cup almond flour

1. Coat a slow cooker generously with cooking spray.

2. Place the berries on the bottom of the slow cooker and sprinkle them with 2 tablespoons of erythritol.

3. In a large bowl, mix together the egg, coconut oil, remaining 1 tablespoon erythritol, and the vanilla. Fold in the coconut flour and the almond flour, mixing well until a thick batter forms.

4. Spread the batter evenly on top of the berries with the back of a spoon or your hand and press it down lightly.

5. Place a paper towel between the slow cooker and the lid to cut down on any condensation that develops. Cook on low for 4 to 6 hours or on high for 2 to 3 hours, or until a toothpick inserted in the center comes out clean.

Substitution tip: This recipe is flexible enough to swap ingredients. Try using blueberries, blackberries, or raspberries, or a mixture of all of them.

PER SERVING: Calories: 287; Fat: 23g; Carbohydrates: 16g; Fiber: 7g; Protein: 7g; Sodium: 19mg

Gingerbread

Serves 12 / **Prep time:** 10 minutes / **Cook time:** 3 hours on low

Gingerbread is a traditional favorite in the winter months because the spices are delicious and have been proven to support a healthy immune system. This recipe is ideal for making in a 3.5-quart slow cooker, if you have one. It comes out with a wonderfully light texture. Try topping the cake with whipped coconut cream for a New Year's Day brunch, festive wedding, or birthday.

Cooking spray

2 cups almond flour

¾ cup powdered erythritol sweetener of your choice

2 tablespoons coconut flour

2 tablespoons ground ginger

2 teaspoons baking powder

2 teaspoons ground cinnamon

½ teaspoon ground nutmeg

¼ teaspoon ground cloves

Pinch salt

¾ cup heavy (whipping) cream

½ cup butter, melted

4 eggs

1 teaspoon pure vanilla extract

1. Coat a slow cooker generously with cooking spray.
2. In a large bowl, stir together the almond flour, erythritol, coconut flour, ginger, baking powder, cinnamon, nutmeg, cloves, and salt.
3. In a medium bowl, whisk together the cream, butter, eggs, and vanilla.
4. Add the wet ingredients to the dry ingredients and stir to combine.
5. Spoon the batter into the insert.
6. Cover and cook on low for 3 hours, or until a toothpick inserted in the center comes out clean.
7. Serve warm.

Ingredient Tip: The spices in this cake create a strongly flavored dessert with a bit of heat from the dried ginger. If you want a slightly mellower dessert, substitute 3 tablespoons of grated fresh ginger instead.

PER SERVING: Calories: 259; Fat: 23g; Carbohydrates: 6g; Fiber: 3g; Protein: 7g; Sodium: 15mg

Vegetable Broth, page 120

broths, stocks & sauces

Vegetable Broth

Makes 8 cups / **Prep time:** 10 minutes / **Cook time:** 8 to 10 hours on low / 4 to 5 hours on high

This vegan broth can be used in pretty much any recipe regardless of a person's dietary restrictions. I like to use "last leg" vegetables when making this broth. You know what I mean—those older carrots or celery stalks in your produce drawer that are one or two days away from having to be thrown out. They might not be pretty enough to serve on their own, but they are great for broth.

8 cups water

4 carrots, sliced

3 celery stalks, sliced

3 large onions, diced

4 garlic cloves, minced

¼ cup fresh parsley

4 sprigs thyme or rosemary

3 bay leaves

½ teaspoon whole black peppercorns

1. Add the water, carrots, celery, onions, garlic, parsley, thyme or rosemary, bay leaves, and peppercorns to a slow cooker.

2. Cook on low for 8 to 10 hours or on high for 4 to 5 hours.

3. Strain the vegetables from the broth using a mesh strainer over a large bowl.

4. Using the back of a spoon, press out the excess liquid from the vegetables through the strainer. Discard the solids.

Make-ahead tip: Store the broth in a covered container in the refrigerator for up to 5 days or freeze for up to 6 months.

PER SERVING (1 CUP): Calories: 15; Fat: g; Carbohydrates: 3g; Fiber: 1g; Protein: 0g; Sodium: 81mg

Bone Broth

Makes 8 cups / **Prep time:** 10 minutes / **Cook time:** 20 to 24 hours on low / 10 to 12 hours on high

The very long cooking time gives this wonderful broth the hours it needs to extract every drop of nutritional value from the bones. You can use two different types of bones here: *jointy* bones, which are cartilage-rich, like wings and necks, or *meaty* bones, like ribs or marrow bones. I like to use a mix of the two.

4 pounds bones

8 cups water

4 celery stalks, sliced

4 carrots, sliced

2 onions, chopped

5 garlic cloves, minced

¼ cup white vinegar

½ teaspoon salt

½ teaspoon freshly ground black pepper

1 bay leaf

1. Add the bones, water, celery, carrots, onions, garlic, vinegar, salt, pepper, and bay leaf to a slow cooker.

2. Cook on low for 20 to 24 hours or on high for 10 to 12 hours.

3. Strain the broth using a large mesh strainer over a large bowl.

Ingredient tip: If you use bones with lots of cartilage or connecting tissue, which is rich in collagen, your broth will start to gel as it cools. But if your bone broth doesn't gel, that's okay. It is still full of important minerals and amino acids, though it might be a bit lower in protein.

Make-ahead tip: Store this bone broth in the refrigerator for up to 3 or 4 days or in the freezer for up to a year.

PER SERVING (1 CUP): Calories: 41; Fat: 1g; Carbohydrates: 6g; Fiber: 1g; Protein: 2g; Sodium: 81mg

Chicken Stock

Makes 8 cups / **Prep time:** 10 minutes / **Cook time:** 8 to 10 hours on low / 4 to 5 hours on high

Save your chicken bones. They can be used to make this incredibly easy and healthy homemade chicken stock. Even better: You can reuse those same bones to make a second batch of stock.

4 pounds chicken bones

8 cups water

5 celery stalks, sliced

5 carrots, sliced

2 large onions, sliced

5 garlic cloves, minced

¼ cup fresh parsley

Pinch salt

Pinch freshly ground black pepper

1. Add the bones, water, celery, carrots, onions, garlic, parsley, salt, and pepper to a slow cooker.

2. Cook on low for 8 to 10 hours or on high for 4 to 5 hours.

3. Strain the broth using a large mesh strainer over a large bowl.

Make-ahead tip: Store the stock in a covered container in the refrigerator for up to 5 days or freeze for up to 6 months.

Ingredient tip: Substitute turkey bones for chicken. Follow the recipe as written.

PER SERVING (1 CUP): Calories: 86; Fat: 3g; Carbohydrates: 8g; Fiber: 2g; Protein: 6g; Sodium: 430mg

Seafood Stock

Makes 4 cups / **Prep time:** 10 minutes / **Cook time:** 8 to hours on low / 4 to 5 hours on high

Seafood stock is wonderful in so many recipes: sauces, gumbos, stews, and so many more. Use any shellfish shells you like, whether shrimp, lobster, crab, or a combination.

Shells from 1 pound of shellfish

2 cups chopped onions

2 carrots, chopped

2 celery stalks, chopped

½ cup low-sodium broth or water

2 garlic cloves, minced

2 tablespoons extra-virgin olive oil

1½ teaspoons salt

1½ teaspoons freshly ground black pepper

5 sprigs thyme

1 bay leaf

1. Add the seafood shells, onions, carrots, celery, broth, garlic, olive oil, salt, pepper, thyme, and bay leaf to the slow cooker. Add enough water to cover all the ingredients.

2. Cook on low for 8 to 10 hours or on high for 4 to 5 hours.

3. Strain the stock into a mesh strainer over a large bowl.

4. Using the back of a spoon, press out the excess liquid from the vegetables and shells through the strainer.

Make-ahead tip: Store the stock in a covered container in the refrigerator for up to 3 to 5 days or freeze for up to 6 months.

PER SERVING (1 CUP): Calories: 10; Fat: 0g; Carbohydrates: 1g; Fiber: 0g; Protein: 0g; Sodium: 872mg

Alfredo Sauce

Makes 4 cups / **Prep time:** 5 minutes / **Cook time:** 8 to 10 hours on low / 4 to 5 hours on high

This creamy sauce can be enjoyed as a topping over zoodles (zucchini noodles) or spaghetti squash and spooned over meats and seafood, as well. The sauce is low-carb but it still has all the delicious cheesy Alfredo flavor we all love.

2 cups heavy (whipping) cream

1½ cups shredded Parmesan cheese

½ cup unsalted butter

3 ounces low-fat cream cheese

2 garlic cloves, minced

Pinch salt

Pinch black pepper

1. Add the heavy cream, Parmesan, butter, cream cheese, garlic, salt, and pepper to a slow cooker. Stir to mix well.

2. Cook on low for 8 to 10 hours or on high for 4 to 5 hours.

3. Transfer the mixture to a food processor or a blender and process until smooth.

Ingredient tip: If the sauce seems on the watery side when it's done, don't worry. It will thicken up as it cools, and it will become very thick when it's stored in the refrigerator.

Make-ahead tip: Store this sauce in your refrigerator for up 3 days.

PER SERVING (1/3 CUP): Calories: 260; Fat: 26g; Carbohydrates: 2g; Fiber: 0g; Protein: 6g; Sodium: 401mg

BBQ Sauce

Makes 4 cups / **Prep time:** 5 minutes / **Cook time:** 6 to 8 hours on low / 3 to 4 hours on high

Finding high-quality, lower-carb store-bought barbecue sauce isn't easy. And when you do find it, its taste is not the best. This version contains erythritol, a natural sweetener found in health food stores and online, and you'll find that it gives you all the sweetness you are looking for in a barbecue sauce.

3¾ cups tomato paste

1¾ cups water (plus more as needed)

1 cup apple cider vinegar

⅔ cup powdered erythritol sweetener of your choice

3 tablespoons Worcestershire sauce

3 tablespoons paprika

2 tablespoons liquid smoke

2 teaspoons garlic powder

1 teaspoon onion powder

1 teaspoon salt

½ teaspoon chili powder

1. Add the tomato paste, water, vinegar, erythritol, Worcestershire sauce, paprika, liquid smoke, garlic powder, onion powder, salt, and chili powder to a slow cooker. Stir to mix well.

2. Cook on low for 6 to 8 hours or on high for 3 to 4 hours.

3. Transfer the mixture to a food processor or a blender and process until smooth. Add more water if needed for your desired consistency.

Make-ahead tip: Store the sauce in a covered container in your refrigerator for up to a month.

PER SERVING (2 TABLESPOONS): Calories: 24; Fat: 0g; Carbohydrates: 6g; Fiber: 2g; Protein: 1g; Sodium: 100mg

Cheese Sauce

Makes 6 cups / **Prep time:** 5 minutes / **Cook time:** 2 to 4 hours on low / 1 to 2 hours on high

A good cheese sauce enhances just about anything. Whatever you pour it on—vegetables, meats, or even a salad as a light dressing—is going to taste great.

4 cups heavy (whipping) cream

1 pound sharp Cheddar cheese, shredded

Pinch salt

Pinch black pepper

1. Add the cream, cheese, salt, and pepper to a slow cooker. Stir to mix well.

2. Cook on low for 2 to 4 hours or on high for 1 to 2 hours, or until the cheese is melted.

3. Once cooled, transfer the sauce to a food processor or a blender and process until smooth.

Make-ahead tip: Store the leftover sauce in a covered container in the refrigerator for up to 4 days. If it's too thick after you've reheated it, add a little cream and cook over low heat until hot.

PER SERVING (1/4 CUP): Calories: 96; Fat: 7g; Carbohydrates: 2g; Fiber: 0g; Protein: 6g; Sodium: 151mg

Chimichurri Sauce

Makes 2 cups / **Prep time:** 5 minutes / **Cook time:** 6 hours on low / 3 hours on high

Chimichurri is a sauce used in South American and Mexican cooking. It isn't usually cooked, but I discovered that slow cooking the ingredients enhanced the flavors, so that's how I always make it now. You will love this sauce on steak, seafood, or poultry.

2 cups fresh parsley leaves (see Ingredient tip)

1 cup extra-virgin olive oil

⅔ cup red wine vinegar

½ cup fresh cilantro

4 garlic cloves, peeled

1 teaspoon red pepper flakes

1 teaspoon ground cumin

½ teaspoon salt

1. Add the parsley, olive oil, vinegar, cilantro, garlic, red pepper flakes, cumin, and salt to the slow cooker. Stir to mix well.

2. Cook on low for 6 hours or on high for 3 hours. Let cool.

3. Transfer the cooled mixture to a food processor and pulse until it becomes a rough paste.

Ingredient tip: For the cilantro, it's fine to use the stems and leaves in this sauce, but for parsley, use only the leaves. The stems are tougher and they can make the sauce bitter.

Make-ahead tip: Store this in the refrigerator for up to 3 days.

PER SERVING (2 TABLESPOONS): Calories: 127; Fat: 14g; Carbohydrates: 2g; Fiber: 0g; Protein: 0g; Sodium: 78mg

Cream of Mushroom Sauce

Makes 4 cups / **Prep time:** 10 minutes / **Cook time:** 8 to 10 hours on low / 4 to 5 hours on high

Yes, I've called this a sauce, but go ahead and serve this as a soup, too. I prefer to use it as an ingredient, which is why I've placed it in this chapter. It will be pretty thick, but if you want to eat it on its own as soup, add a little water or vegetable broth and reheat it before serving.

1 pound mushrooms, chopped

3 cups Vegetable Broth (page 120) or store-bought low-sodium vegetable broth

1 small onion, chopped

1 cup 2% reduced-fat milk

4 ounces low-fat cream cheese

¼ cup unsalted butter

1 garlic clove, minced

½ teaspoon salt

½ teaspoon freshly ground black pepper

¼ teaspoon thyme

1. Add the mushrooms, broth, onion, milk, cream cheese, butter, garlic, salt, pepper, and thyme to a slow cooker. Stir to mix well.

2. Cook on low for 8 to 10 hours or on high for 4 to 5 hours.

3. Once cooled, transfer the mixture to a food processor or a blender and process until smooth.

Make it faster: Add all the ingredients to an Instant Pot, stir well, lock the lid, and pressure cook on Manual for 10 minutes. Release the pressure naturally.

PER SERVING (1 CUP): Calories: 234; Fat: 18g; Carbohydrates: 13g; Fiber: 2g; Protein: 8g; Sodium: 527mg

Ghee

Makes 4 cups / **Prep time:** 5 minutes / **Cook time:** 4 to 6 hours on low / 2 to 3 hours on high

Ghee is simply clarified butter (butter with the milk solids removed), and it's an ingredient widely used in Indian cuisine. Store-bought ghee can be expensive, so I recommend making it yourself, and it's even easier when you use a slow cooker. Ghee will be a golden color when it finishes cooking, and as it cools, it will solidify. For this recipe you'll also need cheesecloth or coffee filters and a mesh strainer.

2 pounds unsalted butter

1. Add the butter to a slow cooker. Leave the lid slightly ajar to let steam escape.

2. Cook on low for 4 to 6 hours or on high for 2 to 3 hours.

3. Line a strainer with cheesecloth or a coffee filter, and set over a mason jar or a bowl. Carefully pour the liquid through the strainer and discard the solids.

4. Let the ghee cool. Store in a cool, dry place.

Ingredient tip: Ghee will keep at room temperature for 3 months and in the refrigerator for up to 1 year. It can also be frozen and kept indefinitely.

PER SERVING (1 TABLESPOON): Calories: 95; Fat: 11g; Carbohydrates: 0g; Fiber: 0g; Protein: 0g; Sodium: 2mg

Ketchup

Makes 4 cups / **Prep time:** 5 minutes / **Cook time:** 4 to 6 hours on low / 2 to 3 hours on high

Store-bought ketchup is usually packed with added sugar and some not-so-low-carb-friendly ingredients I can barely pronounce. While this version is lower in carbs than commercial ketchups, you will never know it after you taste it.

2 cups low-sodium or no-salt-added tomato sauce

¼ cup apple cider vinegar

1 small onion, diced

2 garlic cloves, minced

1 tablespoon of powdered erythritol sweetener of your choice

1 tablespoon ground mustard

1 teaspoon salt

½ teaspoon Worcestershire sauce

¼ teaspoon freshly ground black pepper

¼ teaspoon cinnamon

¼ teaspoon paprika

1. Add the tomato sauce, vinegar, onion, garlic, erythritol, mustard, salt, Worcestershire sauce, pepper, cinnamon, and paprika to a slow cooker. Stir to mix well.

2. Cook on low for 4 to 6 hours or on high for 2 to 3 hours.

3. Once cooled, transfer the mixture to a blender and purée the sauce to your desired consistency.

Ingredient tip: If you like your ketchup on the sweeter side, add ½ teaspoon or more of erythritol.

Make-ahead tip: Store in a covered container in the refrigerator for up to 3 weeks.

PER SERVING (2 TABLESPOONS): Calories: 6; Fat: 0g; Carbohydrates: 2g; Fiber: 0g; Protein: 0g; Sodium: 76mg

Strawberry Sauce

Makes 1½ to 2 cups / Prep time: 5 minutes / **Cook time:** 4 to 6 hours on low / 2 to 3 hours on high

For breakfast, spoon this sauce over Greek yogurt, or try it for dessert over slices of a low-carb cake. You can also make this with other berries, like blueberries, raspberries, or blackberries.

2 cups diced fresh strawberries

1 teaspoon powdered erythritol sweetener of your choice

¼ teaspoon vanilla extract

1. Add the strawberries, erythritol, and vanilla to a slow cooker. Stir to mix well.

2. Cook on low for 4 to 6 hours or on high for 2 to 3 hours.

3. Transfer the mixture to a food processor or a blender and process until smooth.

Ingredient tip: Raspberries and blackberries are the best alternate berry choices in terms of keeping the carbs low.

Make-ahead tip: Store in your refrigerator for up to 3 days or freeze for up to 3 months.

PER SERVING: Calories: 18; Fat: 0g; Carbohydrates: 5g; Fiber: 1g; Protein: 0g; Sodium: 1mg

MEASUREMENT CONVERSIONS

Volume Equivalents (Liquid)

STANDARD	US STANDARD (OUNCES)	METRIC (APPROXIMATE)
2 tablespoons	1 fl. oz.	30 mL
¼ cup	2 fl. oz.	60 mL
½ cup	4 fl. oz.	120 mL
1 cup	8 fl. oz.	240 mL
1½ cups	12 fl. oz.	355 mL
2 cups or 1 pint	16 fl. oz.	475 mL
4 cups or 1 quart	32 fl. oz.	1 L
1 gallon	128 fl. oz.	4 L

Oven Temperatures

FAHRENHEIT (F)	CELSIUS (C) (APPROXIMATE)
250°	120°
300°	150°
325°	165°
350°	180°
375°	190°
400°	200°
425°	220°
450°	230°

Volume Equivalents (Dry)

STANDARD	METRIC (APPROXIMATE)
⅛ teaspoon	0.5 mL
¼ teaspoon	1 mL
½ teaspoon	2 mL
¾ teaspoon	4 mL
1 teaspoon	5 mL
1 tablespoon	15 mL
¼ cup	59 mL
⅓ cup	79 mL
½ cup	118 mL
⅔ cup	156 mL
¾ cup	177 mL
1 cup	235 mL
2 cups or 1 pint	475 mL
3 cups	700 mL
4 cups or 1 quart	1 L

Weight Equivalents

STANDARD	METRIC (APPROXIMATE)
½ ounce	15 g
1 ounce	30 g
2 ounces	60 g
4 ounces	115 g
8 ounces	225 g
12 ounces	340 g
16 ounces or 1 pound	455 g

THE DIRTY DOZEN™ AND THE CLEAN FIFTEEN™

A nonprofit environmental watchdog organization called Environmental Working Group (EWG) looks at data supplied by the U.S. Department of Agriculture (USDA) and the Food and Drug Administration (FDA) about pesticide residues. Each year it compiles a list of the best and worst pesticide loads found in commercial crops. You can use these lists to decide which fruits and vegetables to buy organic to minimize your exposure to pesticides and which produce is considered safe enough to buy conventionally. This does not mean they are pesticide-free, though, so wash these fruits and vegetables thoroughly.

Dirty Dozen™

Apples	Pears
Celery	Potatoes
Cherries	Spinach
Grapes	Strawberries
Nectarines (imported)	Sweet bell peppers
Peaches	Tomatoes

Additionally, nearly three-quarters of hot pepper samples contained pesticide residues

Clean Fifteen™

Asparagus	Kiwi
Avocados	Mangos
Broccoli	Onions
Cabbages	Papayas
Cantaloupe	Pineapples
Cauliflower	Sweet corn
Eggplant	Sweet peas (frozen)
Honeydew melon	

RECIPE INDEX

INDEX

ACKNOWLEDGMENTS

Thank you to my husband for not only supporting me through writing another cookbook, but for also being my guinea pig and eating lots of low-carb slow cooker recipes. To Callisto—you guys are the best. A special thank you to my "co-writing" team: nutritionist Deanna Segrave-Daly and editor Amy Treadwell. Thanks as well to Elizabeth Castoria for once again putting this opportunity on my plate; Stacy Wagner-Kinnear for championing this book from the very beginning; editors Erum Khan and Edgar Doolan; and everyone behind the scenes that helped make this possible.

ABOUT THE AUTHOR

 **Shannon Epstein** is a full-time food and travel writer. She is the author of *The Easy and Healthy Slow Cooker Cookbook* and has two blogs, FitSlowCookerQueen (healthy slow cooker recipes) and TweetEatTravel (travel and lifestyle). Shannon lives in Los Angeles with her husband.